First World War
and Army of Occupation
War Diary
France, Belgium and Germany

2 DIVISION
19 Infantry Brigade
Royal Welsh Fusiliers
2nd Battalion
4 August 1914 - 30 November 1915

WO95/1365/3

The Naval & Military Press Ltd
www.nmarchive.com
Published in association with The National Archives

Published by

The Naval & Military Press Ltd

Unit 10 Ridgewood Industrial Park,

Uckfield, East Sussex,

TN22 5QE England

Tel: +44 (0) 1825 749494

www.naval-military-press.com

www.nmarchive.com

This diary has been reprinted in facsimile from the original. Any imperfections are inevitably reproduced and the quality may fall short of modern type and cartographic standards.

© **Crown Copyright**
Images reproduced by permission of The National Archives, London, England, 2015.

Contents

Document type	Place/Title	Date From	Date To
Heading	WO95/1365/3		
Heading	2 Division 19 Bde 2 Bn R Welsh Fus 1914 Aug-1915 Nov		
Heading	19th Infantry Brigade 2nd Battalion Royal Welsh Fusiliers August 1914		
War Diary	Portland	04/08/1914	08/08/1914
War Diary	Dorchester	10/08/1914	10/08/1914
War Diary	Southampton	11/08/1914	11/08/1914
War Diary	Ronen	12/08/1914	22/08/1914
War Diary	Valenciennes	23/08/1914	23/08/1914
War Diary	Vicq	24/08/1914	24/08/1914
War Diary	Jenlain	25/08/1914	25/08/1914
War Diary	Le Cateau	26/08/1914	26/08/1914
War Diary	Ollezy	28/08/1914	28/08/1914
War Diary	Pontoise	29/08/1914	30/08/1914
War Diary	Couloisy	31/08/1914	31/08/1914
Miscellaneous	Questions About Part Played By The 2nd Batt Rgt In 1914		
Heading	19th Infantry Brigade 2nd Battalion Royal Welsh Fusiliers September 1914		
War Diary	3M.S Of La Croix S of Forest of Campiegnie	01/09/1914	01/09/1914
War Diary	Nr Fresnoy	02/09/1914	02/09/1914
War Diary	Dammartin	03/09/1914	03/09/1914
War Diary	Lagny	04/09/1914	05/09/1914
War Diary	Grisy	06/09/1914	06/09/1914
War Diary	St Dennis	07/09/1914	07/09/1914
War Diary	La Haute Maison	08/09/1914	08/09/1914
War Diary	La Ferte Sous Jouarre	09/09/1914	09/09/1914
War Diary	Les Corbiere	10/09/1914	10/09/1914
War Diary	Certigny	11/09/1914	11/09/1914
War Diary	St Genevieve	12/09/1914	12/09/1914
War Diary	Burancy	13/09/1914	13/09/1914
War Diary	La Carriere L'Eve'Que	14/09/1914	14/09/1914
War Diary	S.E Of Venizel	15/09/1914	19/09/1914
War Diary	Septmonts	20/09/1914	30/09/1914
Heading	19th Infantry Brigade 2nd Battalion Royal Welsh Fusiliers October 1914		
War Diary	Septmonts	01/10/1914	05/10/1914
War Diary	St Remy	06/10/1914	06/10/1914
War Diary	Vez	07/10/1914	07/10/1914
War Diary	Longveill St Marie	08/10/1914	08/10/1914
War Diary	Estrees St Dennis	09/10/1914	11/10/1914
War Diary	Renesare	12/10/1914	15/10/1914
War Diary	Vlamertinghe	16/10/1914	19/10/1914
War Diary	Laventie	20/10/1914	20/10/1914
War Diary	Fromelles	21/10/1914	21/10/1914
War Diary	La Boutillerie	22/10/1914	31/10/1914
Heading	19th Infantry Brigade 2nd Battalion Royal Welsh Fusiliers November 1914		
War Diary	La Boutillerie Fromelles	01/11/1914	14/11/1914

War Diary	Sailly	15/11/1914	17/11/1914
War Diary	Houplines	18/11/1914	30/11/1914
Heading	19th Brigade 2nd Battalion Royal Welsh Fusiliers December 1914		
War Diary	Houplines	01/12/1914	02/12/1914
War Diary	Nr. Frelinghiem	03/12/1914	25/12/1914
War Diary	Nr. Erquinhiem	26/12/1914	31/12/1914
Miscellaneous	Extract from Letter of the Late 2/Lieutenant M.S. Richardson	25/12/1914	25/12/1914
Heading	19th Inf Bde 6th Div War Diary 2nd Battn The Royal Welsh Fusiliers January 1915		
War Diary	Erquinghem	01/01/1915	01/01/1915
War Diary	Gris Pot	02/01/1915	07/01/1915
War Diary	Nr. Bois Grenier	08/01/1915	18/01/1915
War Diary	Gris Pot	19/01/1915	23/01/1915
War Diary	Nr. Bois Grenier	24/01/1915	29/01/1915
War Diary	Gris-pot	30/01/1915	31/01/1915
Heading	19th Inf Bde 6th Div War Diary 2nd Battn The Royal Welsh Fusiliers February 1915		
War Diary	Gris-pot	01/02/1915	02/02/1915
War Diary	Nr. Bois Grenier	03/02/1915	07/02/1915
War Diary	Gris-pot	08/02/1915	12/02/1915
War Diary	Nr. Bois Grenier	13/02/1915	17/02/1915
War Diary	Gris-pot	18/02/1915	22/02/1915
War Diary	Nr. Bois Grenier	23/02/1915	27/02/1915
War Diary	Gris-pot	28/02/1915	28/02/1915
Heading	19th Inf Bde 6th Div War Diary 2nd Battn The Royal Welsh Fusiliers March 1915		
War Diary	Gris-pot	01/03/1915	04/03/1915
War Diary	Nr. Bois Grenier	05/03/1915	09/03/1915
War Diary	Gris-pot	10/03/1915	12/03/1915
War Diary	L'armee	13/03/1915	14/03/1915
War Diary	Nr La Vesee	15/03/1915	20/03/1915
War Diary	L'Armee	21/03/1915	22/03/1915
War Diary	Gris-pot	23/03/1915	25/03/1915
War Diary	Nr. La Vesee	26/03/1915	30/03/1915
War Diary	Gris-pot	31/03/1915	31/03/1915
Heading	19th Inf Bde 6th Div War Diary 2nd Battn The Royal Welsh Fusiliers April 1915		
War Diary	Gris-pot	01/04/1915	03/04/1915
War Diary	Nr. Bois Grenier	04/04/1915	09/04/1915
War Diary	Gris pot	10/04/1915	14/04/1915
War Diary	Nr. Bois Grenier	15/04/1915	19/04/1915
War Diary	Gris pot	20/04/1915	24/04/1915
War Diary	Nr. Bois Grenier	25/04/1915	29/04/1915
War Diary	Gris pot	30/04/1915	30/04/1915
Heading	19th Inf Bde 6th Div War Diary 2nd Battn. The Royal Welsh Fusiliers May 1915		
War Diary	Gris-pot	01/05/1915	04/05/1915
War Diary	Nr. Bois Grenier	05/05/1915	09/05/1915
War Diary	Gris-pot	10/05/1915	14/05/1915
War Diary	Nr. Bois Grenier	15/05/1915	20/05/1915
War Diary	Gris-pot	21/05/1915	26/05/1915
War Diary	Nr. Bois Grenier	27/05/1915	31/05/1915
Heading	27th Division 19th Infy Bde 2nd Bn Roy Welsh Fus Jun-Jly 1915		

Heading	19th Infantry Brigade 27th Division War Diary 2nd Battn The Royal Welsh Fusiliers June 1915			
War Diary	Gris-pot	01/06/1915	01/06/1915
War Diary	Nr. La Vesee	02/06/1915	08/06/1915
War Diary	Gris-pot	09/06/1915	10/06/1915
War Diary	Nr. Bois Grenier	11/06/1915	16/06/1915
War Diary	Gris-pot	17/06/1915	18/06/1915
War Diary	Rue Du Bois	19/06/1915	24/06/1915
War Diary	Gris-pot	25/06/1915	29/06/1915
War Diary	Nr. Bois Grenier	30/06/1915	30/06/1915
Heading	19th Infantry Brigade 27th Division War Diary 2nd Battn The Royal Welsh Fusiliers July 1915			
War Diary	Nr. Bois Grenier	01/07/1915	04/07/1915
War Diary	Gris-pot	05/07/1915	09/07/1915
War Diary	Nr. Bois Grenier	10/07/1915	14/07/1915
War Diary	Gris-pot	15/07/1915	19/07/1915
War Diary	W Steenwerck	20/07/1915	23/07/1915
War Diary	Fauquissart	24/07/1915	29/07/1915
War Diary	Laventie	30/07/1915	31/07/1915
Heading	2nd Division 19th Infy Bde 2nd Battalion Royal Welsh Fusiliers Aug-Nov 1915 To 33 Div 19 Bde			
Heading	19th Infantry Brigade 2nd Division War Diary 2nd Battn The Royal Welsh Fusiliers August 1915			
War Diary	Laventie	01/08/1915	04/08/1915
War Diary	Nr. Rue Tilleloy	05/08/1915	10/08/1915
War Diary	Laventie	11/08/1915	15/08/1915
War Diary	Nr. Doulieu Vieux Berquin	16/08/1915	18/08/1915
War Diary	Bethune	19/08/1915	23/08/1915
War Diary	Cuinchy	24/08/1915	27/08/1915
War Diary	Annequin	28/08/1915	29/08/1915
War Diary	Cuinchy	30/08/1915	31/08/1915
Heading	19th Infantry Brigade 2nd Division War Diary 2nd Battn. The Royal Welsh Fusiliers September 1915			
War Diary	Cuinchy	01/09/1915	02/09/1915
War Diary	Annequin	03/09/1915	04/09/1915
War Diary	Bethune	05/09/1915	13/09/1915
War Diary	Givenchy	14/09/1915	17/09/1915
War Diary	Bethune	18/09/1915	20/09/1915
War Diary	Maison Rouge	21/09/1915	23/09/1915
War Diary	Bethune	24/09/1915	24/09/1915
War Diary	Cambrin	25/09/1915	30/09/1915
Heading	19th Infantry Brigade 2nd Division War Diary 2nd Battn The Royal Welsh Fusiliers October 1915			
War Diary	Cambrin	01/10/1915	01/10/1915
War Diary	Sailly La Bourse	02/10/1915	02/10/1915
War Diary	Annezin	03/10/1915	15/10/1915
War Diary	Bethune	16/10/1915	19/10/1915
War Diary	Cambrin	20/10/1915	24/10/1915
War Diary	Annequin	25/10/1915	28/10/1915
War Diary	Busnettes	29/10/1915	31/10/1915
Heading	19th Infantry Brigade 2nd Division War Diary 2nd Battn The Royal Welsh Fusiliers November 1915			
War Diary	Busnettes	01/11/1915	04/11/1915
War Diary	Bethune	05/11/1915	05/11/1915
War Diary	Cambrin	06/11/1915	18/11/1915
War Diary	Beuvry	19/11/1915	20/11/1915

War Diary	Gonnehem	21/11/1915	28/11/1915
War Diary	Oblinghem	29/11/1915	30/11/1915
Heading	19 Infantry Brigade 2 Bn Argyle & Sutherland Highlanders 1 Bn Middlesex Regiment 2 Bn Royal Welsh Fus 1914 Aug To 1915 Nov		

WO 95/13651/3

2 DIVISION

19 BDE

2 BN R WELCH FUS

1914 AUG — 1915 NOV

19th Infantry Brigade.

2nd BATTALION

ROYAL WELCH FUSILIERS

AUGUST 1 9 1 4

2nd Bt Royal Welch Fus.P.

War Diary

Place & Date		Information	Remarks
Ireland	4th August 1914	Orders to mobilise received at 9 p.m.	(1)
"	5th "	20 Officers 550 R & F proceeded to Dovercote	(1)
"	6th "	4 Bn & Mob teested C.O.	(1)
Dovercote	10th "	Return completed mobilization, received & transport moving by road to Dovercote Marsh.	
		29 Officers 1 W.O. 1065 R & F.	(2)
		The Whole moved in two train loads to Southampton	(2)
Southampton	11th "	Hd qrs & A & B Coys Embarked in S.S. "Gengarry" C. & D. to Base Camp	(2)
Rouen	12th "	Sailed from Southampton at 2 a.m. 16 Officers 495 R & F arrived at Rouen 4.30. p.m. & disentrained & were teested to N & S side of R. SEINE	(1)
Rouen	13th "	4 Officers 120 N.C.Os & mers A Coy Entrained at 3 p.m. for AMIENS.	(1)
"	14th "	240 Coys arrived at 7 a.m., remainder of Transport arrived at 7 p.m.	(2)
"	20th "	1 Officer 104 R & F B Coy Entrained for AMIENS at 5 p.m. Orders received to be in readiness to move, all transport, mules etc, at once called in.	(2)

Place	Date	Information	Remarks
Rouen	21st August 1914	Orders received to move to to at GARE DU NORD at 9.25 a.m. 22nd inst.	
"	22nd "	28 Officers & 2 Interpreters 738 16+d, 55 horses, 7 Vehicles entrained at 10.25 a.m. 7 men left in hospital at ROUEN. A Coy. 7 Officers + 227 16+d of 2 Vehicles, 20 horses entrained at AMIENS at 11 p.m. 2 men left in hospital at AMIENS.	
Valenciennes	23rd "	B C + D Coys detrained Valenciennes at about 2 a.m. A Coy arrived at 7 a.m. + detrained. Battalion moved to Onnaing reached about 9. Went to Vicq (8 miles) took up an out-post position on Escaut.	
Vicq	24th "	Orders received 1.10 a.m. to move to Quearoverain. Subsequently advanced ward to Elnys & Thivencelle and took up an entrenched position to etc N.S.B. Battalion retired from there at 11.45 a.m. & took up an entrenched position N of Jenlain Capt d J. Haliagh also wounded & sent into sent to Bros Sep 17. 2 d missing attacked to I D Brigade.	
Jenlain	25th "	Retired from Jenlain at 5 a.m. + marched to Horussy arriving there 10.30 a.m. Took up a position to cover retirement of Middlesex Regt. Eventually retired in Le Cateau. Casualties 18 Sept. 16 missing.	

Place & Date	Information	Remarks
St Julien 26th August 1914	Left St Julien at 3.30 a.m. German cyclists seen in town. Enemy cyclist fought heavy losses in front rides. 6 & 8th XIX Brigade reinforced T Guard then entire retreat of Flank & Cavalry and rest force Rear Guard, retired all night, halting at Estrées sur l'Enver, & eventually arrived at Ollezy. 28 mile march. 6.0 a.m. on 26 & 8/15 14th Brigade on Right. 3rd Division in left. All quiet	(a)
Ollezy 28th August 1914	2 till 9.8 am S. Hospital near Villeveque. Hostile 9.30 am XIX Brigade. formed Rear Guard to 3rd Division to. moved to Noyon 32 miles. Limbs dy arriving at Pontoise about 9 pm.	(a)
Pontoise 29th	In billets at Pontoise re-organising and re-equipping Battalion. Road to the RoD duty at 4 a.m. at Pontoise, nothing occurred.	(b)
" 30th		(a)
Pontoise " 31st	6 a.m. Bridges over Canal + river blown up retired to Jaulzy 14 miles RWF Rear Guard at hostile to close. Bivouacked at 7 a.m. through Forest de Compiègne arrived at Rethondes 4 miles S of La Croix XIX Brigade took up an outpost line. Cavalry outposts by Berman Uhlans, no fighting. Field and drove them off. Attached to IV Dn 19 miles	(a)

Midrid Ridcliffe Lt Col
Commanding 2nd Bn 6/5/F

Questions about part played by the 2nd Battn. R.W.F. in 1914, and provisional answers by me.
Col. H Delmé Radcliffe, then O.C. 2/23rd/19 Bde.

Question 1. Were there any special points to notice about the mobilisation? e.g. had you a large percentage of men with only 3 years Colour Service, among your Reservists?

Answer 1. Some of the orders were not very clear, for instance it was not clear whether we were to proceed from Portland to Dorchester, or straight on to Southampton. This necessitated wiring for instructions, when we got to Dorchester, and then orders came that we were to stop there. When we did stop there we were kept there unnecessarily long, we thought. I forget the number of days now, but will find out. Our men had an uncomfortable time in Dorchester. It would have been better, if we had been kept longer at Portland and had then only gone to Dorchester for 48 hours at the outside. There were also a few other points, which I will give later.

As regards the number of Reservists with 3 years Colour Service I cannot now remember, but think I can get some information about this from Serjeant Major (now Captain) Murphy, who was my Battalion Serjeant Major then. I am going to write to him about it.

Question 2. Can you mark the position of your outpost line taken up near Vicq on August 23rd on the enclosed 100,000 map? Were your outposts in actual touch with the enemy that night?

Answer 2. I can mark the position of my outpost line near Vicq on August 23rd pretty accurately as I put the whole line out myself, and visited every portion of it.

My outpost line was not in actual touch with the enemy that night, though I think a few sniping shots were fired at my outposts. The Middlesex Regiment on the Canal north of us were in touch with the enemy, and had

2.

casualties, including a Major, who I think was killed.

Question 3. Can you mark on the map your route of August 24th and any positions taken up? Did you see any of the fighting round Elouges and Andregnies? Was your Battalion actually in action on this day?

Answer 3. I can mark on the map our route of August 24th fairly accurately. We took up and entrenched a position about midday, but in the afternoon were ordered to march on. We saw our Cavalry in action with the enemy, and also saw the enemy shelling and setting fire to village after village to the North. We were not actually engaged then. At nightfall we entrenched a position at Jenlain, expecting to be attacked, and enemy snipers came up to our position, and, by one of these, Captain Walwyn D.S.O. was wounded in the foot, and had to be put in an Ambulance. No attack actually came off, and we marched on very early on the morning of August 25th, before daylight.

Question 4 Can you mark your route on August 25th? and mark the position taken up by you to cover the retirement of the Middlesex Regiment? Were they being pressed, if so in what force and did you get any targets, while covering them?

Answer 4 I can mark our route of August 25th fairly accurately, also the position taken up to cover the retirement of the Middlesex Regiment. As far as I can remember the Middlesex were not hard pressed, though the Germans were coming on in large numbers, and our move was a precautionary one more than a matter of urgency. Our men got some targets, mostly only at fairly long range. Enemy did not close with us. Later we were shelled by enemy horse batteries

Question 5. About what hour did you reach Le Cateau on August 25th? Can you mark the positions where you spent the night? (billets or bivouacs?) and show the outposts (if any) that you found?

Answer 5. We reached Le Cateau close on 10 p.m. on August 25th, as far as I can remember. We were supposed to billet in the town of Le Cateau ~~[struck through]~~, but we actually practically all bivouacked in the market place (I think it was), some of the men and the officers being in the nearest house entrances, and we only found picquets at the entrances of the streets to the market place, and we patrolled these streets for some distance. As far as I can remember practically the whole Brigade bivouacked in this open square, just as we did.

Question 6. We gather that most of the battalions were in condition to have repeated on August 26th the march of the previous day, but that there must inevitably have been some straggling as so many Reservists were out of condition and footsore. Do you think this would apply to your Battalion? We have formed the impression that the 19th Brigade, hurriedly formed as it was and having been on lines of communication, was even more highly tried than the units who had marched up to Mons from the concentration area. Do you think this is correct? Had you for example been specially badly off as regards getting rations?

Answer 6. My Battalion could certainly have repeated on August 26th the march of August 25th. The thing which was most troublesome to the men was the carrying of the Greatcoats in their valises as the weather was so hot. They certainly never ought to have been carried by the men at that season. There was very little straggling in my Battalion. I certainly think the 19th Brigade must have been at a disadvan-

4.
tage compared to the other Brigades, owing to the number of Reservists we had in the ranks, who had recently re-joined. My Battalion only landed from India in March 1914. We had no difficulty at all about rations till the day of Le Cateau. Here I wish to make two remarks.
(1.) The spirit of my whole Battalion, all ranks, was splendid. There was never a murmur of complaint, and the footsore men, and those tired carrying their packs, stuck it out magnificently.
(2.) I have nothing but praise for the Army Service Corps. I think their efforts to keep the Battalions served with rations, were most self-sacrificing, and the results under the circumstances, highly satisfactory. They deserve the very highest praise, in my opinion.

Question 7.
Was the Battalion actually in contact with the German cyclists, whom your Battalion Diary describes as being seen in Le Cateau, when you moved off at 5.30 a.m.?

Answer 7.
The rear Company of my Battalion may have fired a few shots, but I do not think they did. The Battalion in rear of us, I think it was the Middlesex Regiment, or the A. & S. Highlanders, were certainly in contact with them, and I heard them exchanging shots.

Question 8.
Will you mark the line by which you moved from Le Cateau to the position of Reserve and also mark that position? How long did you remain in position of Reserve?

Answer 8.
I can mark the line by which we moved to the position of Reserve from Le Cateau also that position. I cannot remember off-hand how long we remained in the position of Reserve. General Drummond first took one Battalion away, the Middlesex Regiment, and then the A. & S. Highlanders, and left me in command of the remainder of the Brigade, with orders to send them Battalions to him as called for by him.

5.

Question 9. The Battalion Diary says: "reinforced R. flank, then covered retreat of L. flank. Should not this be the other way on? I make out that you and the Cameronians first moved over to Montigny, ready to assist the 3rd Division to retake Caudry, but were not employed to do this and that you then returned to the right to assist to cover the retreat of the 5th Division. An officer of the Norfolks spoke of retiring through Capt. Phillips' company of your Battalion somewhere near Honnechy. We should be very grateful for confirmation of this, and for any details as to your action on this day or anything you saw of the battle. Could you mark the position taken up by your Battalion as rear-guard and show any other units near you? Did the Germans come near enough to give you a chance of either rifle or machine-gun fire?

Answer 9. The Battalion diary is correct, as you will see by following closely what I am about to say, viz:
On marching out from Le Cateau, General Drummond first formed up the Brigade near a little wood in close order (each Batt.n in Quarter Column). Very soon afterwards he took the Middlesex Regt. away with him towards the right of the battle, which was getting violent. Very soon afterwards he came either here to Body back and took the Argyll and Sutherland Highlanders and a company of the Royal Scots Fusiliers away with him to reinforce the Middlesex or to prolong their Right flank, I forget which. Some time afterwards he sent a message to me to bring up the remaining two Battalions, i.e. my own and the Cameronians, to him. I forget at what time this was, but I took the two Battalions to him as ordered, and on reaching him General Drummond gave orders for the two Battalions to get into "Battle formation", i.e. lines of platoons,

and to remain halted in this formation ready
to reinforce the Middlesex and the Argyll and
Sutherland Highlanders. We remained thus for
some time, I forget how long, and then General
Drummond received an urgent message from Army Head
Quarters in Berthry. He sent for me and told
to march with the Cameronians, and my Batt'n
to Berthry, to get orders there, as we were to
re-inforce the left flank (3rd Division 7th ink).
We marched to Berthry and Sir H. Gen. Smith Dorrien
was there, and I was given orders to go with the
2 Battalions by a line shown me on the map to
Montigny and report myself to the G.O.C. there.
I did so, went a little in front of the Battalions
myself and was met by a Staff officer of the other
Division, who pointed out to me what his G.O.C.
wanted the two Batt'ns to do. Hardly had the
head of the Batt'n reached me when a des-
patch rider arrived with an urgent
message from Army Hd Qrs in Berthry, to say
I was to take the two Batt'ns back to Berthry
at once, as they were urgently required there.
I was standing alone for a few minutes before
the two Battalions reached me, and was sniped
at by some German snipers, so took very good
care to prevent the 2 Batt'ns from showing themselves on high ground, and kept them in a hollow.
We marched back to Berthry and there I received
orders to form a rear-guard, the locality on the ground
being pointed out to me on a map. I arranged then
with Lt. Col. Robertson, Commanding the Cameronians, the respective areas of ground we would cover
and he moved off with his Batt'n and I with mine,
and we took up the respective positions. I can
mark mine on the map. It will thus be seen
that we first moved out with a view to support

7.

ing the troops on the right flank, then were moved over to Montigny to re-inforce the left flank, and finally were allotted the task of rear-guard to cover the retreat from the Le Cateau (I think of the 5th Division).

I believe it to be quite correct that some of the Norfolk Regiment retired through Capt Phillips' Company (C. Company) of my Battalion when in position where I had ~~sent~~ ordered Capt. Phillips to take up a line with his Company. This Company and ~~I~~ another saw large masses of Germans in the distance and was I believe in touch with German advanced troops, as it was just getting dark, but were not seriously engaged and had no good targets. I myself with my glasses saw great masses of Germans, and was surprised that we were not heavily shelled. We were shelled but not heavily, perhaps owing to night coming on.

Note (An unfortunate incident occurred just at nightfall. We had seen numerous little parties of German cavalry scouting about and had fired on several. In the falling dusk, A Company — or rather a platoon of A. Company — opened fire on a party of cavalry, which they took to be Germans. I felt sure they were ours and galloped to A Company, blowing my whistle hard and managed to stop them after a burst of independent rapid fire had been delivered. The cavalry turned out, as I thought them to be, our men, and several had been wounded and some ~~to~~ horses killed and wounded. As far as I can remember none of the cavalrymen were killed, and we brought the survivors along with us as ~~our~~ night was coming on ~~rapidly~~ and we were falling back.)

Question 10. You had an action on August 31st, when on outpost near the railway crossing south of La Croix, in which you drove off a German Cavalry attack. Did you make any prisoners, or

8.

*got identification of the enemy opposed to you?
Were they in any strength? (We are anxious to
find out if we can what German Cavalry were
close up with our troops at this time.)*

One of our Cavalry patrols was driven in by Ger-   Answer 10.
man Cavalry Detachments trying to capture them.
Our cavalry patrol galloped through our line.
A picket of A. Company opened fire on the German cavalry, it being nearly dark then, and
the Germans made away very quickly. I am
not certain how many we accounted for, but
I know we captured one wounded German
cavalry man, who said he belonged to the 8th
German Hussars. (Our Cavalry [I think German cavalry were in force, but] should know strength of Germans)

Did you take any part in the actual fighting on   Question 11.
*September 1st, when the Cavalry Brigade was surprised
at Nery and your Brigade moved to its assistance?*

No. I think it was only the Middlesex Regiment,   Answer 11.
which got engaged there. We were not ordered in
that direction. A little later we were ordered
to take up a position to cover the retreat of the
Baggage convoy etc. We took up a position and
entrenched it, and were not ordered to move on
from it till the afternoon. Our Cavalry were in
action and we saw a certain amount of move-
ment, but were not attacked. Only sniping shots
were fired at us. There was a dense fog early in
the morning, which cleared about 9 a.m. as far as I can
remember, though it may have been earlier.

What sort of opposition did the two companies of   Question 12.
*your Regiment encounter at La Ferté sous Jouarre
when they were sent down to clear that place?*

Major Williams, the second-in-command, was in   Answer 12.
command of the two Companies. He reported meeting
fairly stiff opposition. After nightfall, I think about
8.30 p.m. an order was received, I think from General Wilson, for me to take the remainder of the Battⁿ
down, and I did so. It took some time owing to the steepness

of the ground we had to cover, and its also being very slippery.

Question 13. When you moved up to Flanders in October, you first seem to have encountered the enemy near Steenwercke and have had a good deal of skirmishing. Was the opposition only from Cavalry, or had the enemy any cyclists or Jaegers with them then?

Answer 13. We first encountered the enemy on the Bailleul-Armentieres Road, about 2 miles or so East of Bailleul. We were in action with them all that day. *The enemy had field guns too.* Next day we took Steenwercke by the Brigadier's orders (my Battn., I mean.) D. Company under Capt. Cliff-Hill DSO very neatly intercepted a patrol of mounted Jaegers by means of 2 small patrols from that Company. Only one of the two patrols got engaged but it cut off the Jaegers and in 20 seconds (rapid fire) accounted for every horse and man (I think it was one Officer, 1 Serjeant and 10 men).

Question 14. Could you mark the positions you took up on October 20th and 21st at Fromelles, and also at La Cordonnerie on October 22nd?

Answer 14. Yes, I can mark all these positions clearly.

Question 15. Could you give us any details as to these positions and as to the German attacks on you of October 24th to 26th? We should be very glad to know more as to their formations, tactical methods, the targets they offered and any other details of a tactical nature. Apparently after October 26th they seem to have confined themselves more to shelling and sniping and to have only made a few minor efforts to advance against your lines at night.

Answer 15. I cannot personally give much information about this. I think that good information could be got on these points from Brig. General Stockwell, who was at that time Captain in command of A. Company, Lieut. Col. W. G. Holmes, who was at that time a Lieutenant of C. Company, (Both the Captains of C. Company, Capt. R. N. Phillips and Capt. E. W. Jones-Vaughan were killed) and Major the Hon. C. R. Cleff-Hill DSO, who was then the Captain of D. Company. One of the German methods was to push forward snipers by night and make them entrench quite close to our line (within about 50 yards) and they were picked shots who picked off any head as soon as it showed itself. The snipers in turn were covered by the fire of men in the loopholed houses of Rouges Bancs and Vertongnet, which rendered it difficult to deal with the snipers, and the men in Rouges Bancs and Vertongnet together with the advanced line of entrenched snipers covered the attacking troops when they advanced.

Question 16. Have you any general observations you would feel inclined to make, about the way in which our principles and methods of training etc. stood the test of actual experience of war, e.g. as regards outposts etc.?

Answer 16. Speaking in a general way I think our principles and methods of training stood the test of war well. In answering this question many points could be touched on, but the points which occur to me at the moment are as follows, viz:

1. Our men had had hardly any, if any, training at all as sniper scouts. Very careful training in this work is necessary.

2. In outpost work our men had not had nearly enough training in ruses to deceive the enemy, and in the art of bringing off local small coups, nor in the art of detecting enemy ruses and frustrating them.

3. As regards march training, August 1914 made it clear that troops should never be incumbered with packs. Supplied with a heavy great-coat, in such warm weather, a great coat is superfluous they are necessarily, and impairs their efficiency for rapid action. A Cardigan

19th Infantry Brigade.

2nd BATTALION

ROYAL WELCH FUSILIERS

SEPTEMBER 1 9 1 4

Army Form C. 2118.

Written by
Lt. Colonel
A. Roman Syr.

WAR DIARY
or
INTELLIGENCE SUMMARY.
(Erase heading not required.)

Instructions regarding War Diaries and Intelligence Summaries are contained in F. S. Regs., Part II. and the Staff Manual respectively. Title pages will be prepared in manuscript.

Hour, Date, Place	Summary of Events and Information	Remarks and references to Appendices
3 M. Sot La Croix St Ouen		
CANPIEGNIE 1st Sept 1914	No further disturbances during the night. Retired at 5 a.m. through VERBERIE. Cavalry and Artillery engaged in fighting. Division deployed S.E. N. of MS.F. in fight near RARAX Germans much tracks about 1 p.m. 18 guns and 10 prisoners reported. We retired and remained in a hill near FRESNOY being in reserve to Int. posts (5 miles)	(Sd)
N. FRESNOY 2nd Sept 1914	Retired via DAMMARTIN taking up positions on the new entered in Int-posts withdrew at 11.30 p.m. (14 miles)	(Sd)
DAMMARTIN 3rd Sept 1914.	Retired on LAGNY and went into bivouac about 1 mile to East (22 miles)	(Sd)
LAGNY 4th Sept 1914	Remained in bivouac all day	(Sd)
LAGNY 5th Sept 1914	Left LAGNY and retired to GRISY arriving there at 2 a.m. 9 a.m. went into bivouac and was an outpost.	(Sd)

Army Form C. 2118.

WAR DIARY
or
INTELLIGENCE SUMMARY.
(Erase heading not required.)

Instructions regarding War Diaries and Intelligence Summaries are contained in F.S. Regs., Part II. and the Staff Manual respectively. Title pages will be prepared in manuscript.

Hour, Date, Place	Summary of Events and Information	Remarks and references to Appendices
GRISY 5th Sept. 1914	14 miles. MEDICAL OFFICER and 5 men rejoined. Left GRISY at 6 A.M. and advanced to JOSSIGNY. No pickets in advance billed here in readiness. LIEUT. FRENCH and 95 Rank and File, 1st Reinforcements arrived. Advanced to VILLENEUVE SIDENNIS (billets).	O.O.
ST. DENNIS 7th Sept. 1914	2nd LIEUT. STONE and 23 Rank and File 2nd Reinforcements arrived 4 A.M. Marched at 9.30 A.M. Killed at ROMAIN VILLIERS. Then moved on and eventually came in touch with the enemy at LA HAUTE MAISON (billets). Enemy retired. Bivouacked there the night.	O.O.
LA HAUTE MAISON 8th Sept. 1914	March on at 4 A.M. "A" & "B" Companies left flank Guard. "C" & "D" Companies second to XIX Brigade with the Argyll & Sutherland Highlanders - Advanced line 2 hours then moved off XIX Brigade Advanced Guard. G.O. in Command of Main Body	O.O.

WAR DIARY
or
INTELLIGENCE SUMMARY.

(Erase heading not required.)

Army Form C. 2118.

Hour, Date, Place	Summary of Events and Information	Remarks and references to Appendices
LA-FERTÉ-SOUS-JOUARRE. 9th Sept 1914	Advanced Guard scarcely stalled on reaching SIGNY SIGNETS. Then advanced on LA-FERTÉ-SOUS-JOUARRE. Two Companies took up a position in wooded heights above the town. 'C' & 'D' Companies went down to clear the streets in LA-FERTÉ-SOUS-JOUARRE. Eventually about 4.30 p.m. 'C' & 'D' Companies march down and joined 'C' & 'D' Companies (9 mile?) Enemy rearguard action very hard to locate. fairly heavy Rifle fire. Whilst fighting continued, ordered by East Lancashire Bde to start 4 a.m and ordered to SIGNY-SIGNETS. 2nd Burnie Choze Tell 4 p.m. Casualties, 2/Lieut. E.J.V.C. THOMPSON dangerously wounded in abdomen. 1 man killed. + 12 Rank + File wounded. 2nd LIEUT L.S. LLOYD to Hospital sick. Left SIGNY SIGNETS at 4.30 p.m and moved to LES-CORBIÈRES	G

WAR DIARY or INTELLIGENCE SUMMARY.

Army Form C. 2118.

(Erase heading not required.)

Instructions regarding War Diaries and Intelligence Summaries are contained in F.S. Regs., Part II. and the Staff Manual respectively. Title pages will be prepared in manuscript.

Hour, Date, Place	Summary of Events and Information	Remarks and references to Appendices
LES-CORBIERE 10th Sept 1914	and remained there (8 miles) until 4.30 a.m. when moved through LA-FERTÉ-SOUS-JOUATRE over pontoon bridge, as the main bridge had been blown up and halted at farm one mile North of LIMON for 2 hours. Then moved on and bivouacked at CERTIGNY (3 miles) Picketline & men mounted.	do
CERTIGNY 11th Sept 1914	Moved off in rear of IInd Division at 4 a.m. and marched to MARZY St GÉNÉVIÈVE, where we halted for the night, should have gone to CHOUY, but so the men were not mer through to be pulled there (12 miles)	do
ST GÉNÉVIÈVE 12th Sept 1914	Moved off in rear of IInd Division at 6 a.m. and moved along very to route to eventually billeting at BUZANCY (17 miles) the enemy being all along the line at the crossings of the AISNE.	do
BUZANCY 13th Sept 1914	Moved off at 12.30 p.m. halted at LA CARRIÈRE L'ÉVÊQUE QUE FERME the enemy shelling across the AISNE	do

Army Form C. 2118.

WAR DIARY
or
INTELLIGENCE SUMMARY.
(Erase heading not required.)

Instructions regarding War Diaries and Intelligence Summaries are contained in F. S. Regs., Part II. and the Staff Manual respectively. Title pages will be prepared in manuscript.

Hour, Date, Place	Summary of Events and Information	Remarks and references to Appendices
LA CARRIERE L'EVÊQUE 14th Sept. 1914.	Surrounded there (4 miles). Opened off at 12.45 a.m. and halted about 1 mile south east of VENIZEL. Left at 11.15 a.m. and took up a position North and East of VENIZEL, heavy shelling all day, so casualties excepting one horse killed.	(1)
S.E. of VENIZEL 15th Sept. 1914.	Opened off at 2.15 a.m. and took up a position in rear of Company South East of VENIZEL. CAPT. C.I. STOCKWELL and one man reported. Heavy rain during night. One man wounded.	(b)
S.E. of VENIZEL 16th, 14th, A. + 18th Sept. 1914	Remained in same spot.	(2)
19th Sept. 1914.	Moved from VENIZEL to SEPTMONTS at 1.6 a.m. transport following on after dark. Battalion shelled on road, no casualties.	(3)

Army Form C. 2118.

WAR DIARY
or
INTELLIGENCE SUMMARY.
(Erase heading not required.)

Instructions regarding War Diaries and Intelligence Summaries are contained in F. S. Regs., Part II. and the Staff Manual respectively. Title pages will be prepared in manuscript.

Hour, Date, Place	Summary of Events and Information	Remarks and references to Appendices
SEPTMONTS 20th Sept 1914	2nd LIEUT: DAVIES. 14 transport wagons & 94 horses & Mules. 2nd Detachment moved at 8 a.m. Strength 24 officers & 1115 horses and Mules. Moved off for Bivouac 4 miles East of LA CARRIÈRE L'EVÊQUE at 4.15 a.m. Digging all day returned to Billets at SEPTMONTS at night.	◯
SEPTMONTS 21st Sept 1914	Moved off to LA CARRIÈRE L'EVÊQUE at 4 a.m. Sec digging. Relieved by the Middlesex Regiment at 1 p.m.	◯
SEPTMONTS 22nd Sept 1914	Remained in billets. through inspection of harness, & clothing, etc.	◯
SEPTMONTS 23rd Sept 1914	"C" & "D" Companies furnished for digging at 4 a.m. relieved by "A" & "B" Companies at 1 p.m. 8 men reported (absent) (missing)	◯
SEPTMONTS 24th Sept 1914	Drove a man for farmers, but found none.	◯

Army Form C. 2118.

WAR DIARY
or
INTELLIGENCE SUMMARY.
(Erase heading not required.)

Instructions regarding War Diaries and Intelligence Summaries are contained in F. S. Regs., Part II. and the Staff Manual respectively. Title pages will be prepared in manuscript.

Hour, Date, Place	Summary of Events and Information	Remarks and references to Appendices
SEPTEMBER 25th Sept 1914	Company Parades. 2 men reported missing rejoined	A0
26th Sept 1914	2/LIEUT M.S. RICHARDSON and one man joined. Company Parades. 2 entrenched for reinforcements and supplies.	A0
27th Sept 1914	Ordered to move at 5.30 a.m. to SERCHES arrived 6.30 p.m. Brigade to stand fast. Church Parade 9.30 a.m. 1 man reported missing rejoined, also 1 man left — joined by reinforcements	A0
28th Sept 1914	Barricaded road for Stokes Spurs.	A0
29th Sept 1914	Remained in same place & trench digging	A0
30th Sept 1914	Remained in same place.	A0

Kelvin Radcliffe Lt Col.
Commanding 2nd Bn Royal Welsh Fusiliers

19th Infantry Brigade

2nd BATTALION

ROYAL WELCH FUSILIERS

OCTOBER 1914

WAR DIARY
or
INTELLIGENCE SUMMARY.
(Erase heading not required.)

Army Form C. 2118.

Instructions regarding War Diaries and Intelligence Summaries are contained in F. S. Regs., Part II. and the Staff Manual respectively. Title pages will be prepared in manuscript.

Hour, Date, Place	Summary of Events and Information	Remarks and references to Appendices
Oct 1st SEPTMONTS	to "D" Coy digging	(1)
Oct 2nd 1914 "	Remained in Septmonts	(2)
Oct 3rd 1914 "	"	(3)
Oct 4th 1914 "	Church Parade 9.50 a.m.	(2)
Oct 5th 1914 "	2 "B" Coy digging. Moved at 4.30 p.m. and marched to St Remy (3 mls)	(3) 2/2/3
Oct 6th 1914 St REMY	arrived 2 a.m. bivouacked in wood. Remained there [2 bivouac all day]	(1)
Oct 7th 1914 WEZ	Marched to Wez (11m) bivouacked at 4.10 p.m. Bivouac all day] marched at 6.30 p.m and marched about 1 mile west of BETHISY-ST-PIERRE (11 mls)	(1)
	bivouac in woods. Remained in	(1)
Oct 8th 1914 LONGUEUIL-ST MARE	bivouac in woods. Marched out at 6.30 p.m. Marched through VERBERIE over the OISE to LONGUEIL-ST-MARIE. Billeted & bivouacked there (8m). Captain Gayer went sick	(1)
Oct 9th 1914 ESTRÉES ST-DENNIS	Marched out at 8.30 a.m. and went into bivouac at ESTRÉES ST DENNIS (9 mls)	(3)
Oct 10th 1914 "	Entrained at 6 a.m. "A" & "B" Coys & 2 Coys Manchester Regt. Also a	(1)

Army Form C. 2118.

WAR DIARY
or
INTELLIGENCE SUMMARY.
(Erase heading not required.)

Instructions regarding War Diaries and Intelligence Summaries are contained in F. S. Regs., Part II. and the Staff Manual respectively. Title pages will be prepared in manuscript.

Hour, Date, Place	Summary of Events and Information	Remarks and references to Appendices
Oct 11th 1914	Portion of transport "C" & "D" bags 19 of Field Ambulance and remainder of Fd. & J transport entrained 10 a.m. [proceeded via MONTDIDIER AMIENS ABBEVILLE BOULOGNE CALAIS and] & train arrived at St OMER at 10.64. 2nd train arrived at ARQUES at 6 a.m. and detrained there, the whole Battalion moving to RENESCURE where they halted till 5.30 p.m. then moved into billets (9 miles)	Co
Oct 12th 1914 RENESCURE	moved off at 5 a.m. Battalion left Hd. Qrs. & Guard to VI Division billets at La BREARDE finding two coys picketting. Moved off at 3 p.m. and arrived at St SYLVESTRE. took up an outpost position of 2 N & E of village AVS Highlanders on our right. Cavalry holding a line 3 miles to our front (12 miles)	Co 2/03
Oct 13th 1914	moved off at 4.15 am via La BREARDE to ROUGE CROIX, relief there joining remainder of 19 & B. Bde. from here moved to a position Eastwards 1 mile N.W. of STRAZEELLE in reserve to VI Division. Bivouacked there the night (6 miles)	Co
Oct 14th 1914	moved off at 11.30 a.m. via Rbd L advanced guard to 19 Inf. Bde. Hence	

WAR DIARY
or
INTELLIGENCE SUMMARY.
(Erase heading not required.)

Army Form C. 2118.

Instructions regarding War Diaries and Intelligence Summaries are contained in F. S. Regs., Part II. and the Staff Manual respectively. Title pages will be prepared in manuscript.

Hour, Date, Place	Summary of Events and Information	Remarks and references to Appendices
	On Our Right and Left. Passed through STRAZEELE & BAILLEUL slowly	
	O/a Passing through BAILLEUL obviously unnerved on account	
	so far as RE LENTIVE slight opposition. Brigade ordered to halt.	2/2/3
Oct 13th 1914	"C" & "D" Coys remained in Billets along the BAILLEUL-NIEPPE road.	
	"A" & "B" Coys in Support behind them (2 miles) to westward.	
	"A" & "B" Coys moved down to BAILLEUL-NIEPPE road at 5.30 a.m. "C" & "D" Coys	
	had on reconnaissance towards ~~STEENWERCK~~ eventually reoccupying the	
	line during the enemy attack. H.Q. & "A" Coys moved into the town occupying	
	about 12 noon. STEENWERCK taken on by 17 Bd at 12.30 p.m. and into	
	Bivouac in BAILLEUL. The moved on at 4.45 p.m. moved to STEENWERCK	
	where we bivouacked for the night. C & D Coys had a certain amount of	
	fighting during the day. According to Programme the Casualties are	
	nil.	
Oct 16th 1914 VLAMERTINGHE	Brigade off about 12.45 [via NEUVE-EGLISE KEMMEL & VLAMERTINGHE]	
	(in Buses) and Billeted here.	
Oct 14 1914	Bivouacked in billets all day	

WAR DIARY
or
INTELLIGENCE SUMMARY.
(Erase heading not required.)

Army Form C. 2118.

Instructions regarding War Diaries and Intelligence Summaries are contained in F.S. Regs, Part II. and the Staff Manual respectively. Title pages will be prepared in manuscript.

Hour, Date, Place	Summary of Events and Information	Remarks and references to Appendices
Oct 18th 1914 Vlamertinghe	Lt. Col L/Cpl Roy to have sick remained in our billets all day "A" Coy found the outposts at 4 pm. The Sergts Pte C. Edwards who took Pte J. Jackson Pte "C" Coy awarded the French Decoration "Medaille Militaire" for bravery at La Belle Sou-Jourand.	Q0
Oct 19th 1914 —	moved off at 1.30 p.m. R.M.S. forming our Coy [A.E. Cameron] by Cars, moved via KEMMEL - NEUVE-ÉGLISE - STEENWERCK - ESTAIRES to LAVENTIE arriving about 1.15 a.m. into billets.	Q0
Oct 20th 1914 LAVENTIE	Moved off at 9.30 am entrenched a position from FAVOISSART to RUE sud of FLEURBAIX moved forward at 1.30 pm "A" "B" & "C" Coys taking up a position forward of FROMELLES "D" Coy in Local Reserve Trench taken in our right & left.	Q0 −2/2 3
Oct 21st FROMELLES	"D" Coy moved into position on left of Battalion taking up a position held by the Middlesex Regiment who moved further to the left. A certain amount of shelling. 3 men wounded.	Q0
Oct 22nd 1914 LA BOUTILLERIE	Relieved at 1 am by LA BOUTILLERIE left here at 6 am and took up an entrenched position round LA CORDONNERIE FARM B.D.C.	Q0

WAR DIARY
or
INTELLIGENCE SUMMARY.
(Erase heading not required.)

Army Form C. 2118.

Instructions regarding War Diaries and Intelligence Summaries are contained in F.S. Regs., Part II. and the Staff Manual respectively. Title pages will be prepared in manuscript.

Hour, Date, Place	Summary of Events and Information	Remarks and references to Appendices
	firing line "B" in right middleuse on the left French cavalry on our right	do
Oct 23rd 1914 LA BOUTILLERIE	At trenches all day. Occasional amount of sniping and shelling of men	do
Oct 24th 1914	Pte Heppenstalls [Digging] killed	
	At trenches. Slight attack in the morning. Continuous sniping and shelling all day though attacks at 6.30 p.m. Enemy held back. Casualties: W.E.T. Jones wounded. R.J. Pelles & wounded 14.	do
Oct 25th 1914	Attacked at 1.15 a.m. & 4 a.m. both attacks driven off heavily	do 2/2 3
	Shelled all morning. Also attacked several times Casualties: W.IR.P. Wire Pelled. R.J. 10 wounded. R.J. 23.	do
Oct 26th 1914	"C"s 10 days leave. attacked during the early morning. Continued sniping and shelling all through the day. Casualties: Captain F.H. Jones Yaughen "A" & P. Staff killed. Hurt	do
	Rfy. & Unlish wounded. Lt H. Clem. Ratcliffe Strand east. Hrs killed 12 wounded 28.	
Oct 27th 1914	Enemy believed slightly further back. Sniping and shelling Continued	do

WAR DIARY
or
INTELLIGENCE SUMMARY.
(Erase heading not required.)

Army Form C. 2118.

Hour, Date, Place	Summary of Events and Information	Remarks and references to Appendices
Oct 28th LA BOUTILLERIE	Front of the night. Casualties. 2/Lt Parker wounded. R.I. 4 killed 8 wounded. Reinforcements 50 R.I.	(1)
Oct 29th "	Sniping and shelling most of the day. 2 of our men killed by shell fire. Casualties R.I. 2 killed 30 wounded.	(1)
Oct 30th "	Attacked 2 a.m. & 4 a.m. A good deal of shelling as usual. 2/Lt Holmes wounded. R.I. 2 killed 15 wounded.	(1)
Oct 31st	Attacked from 12 midnight to 5 a.m. Enemy repulsed with loss R.I. reinforcements joined. Casualties. R.I. 2 killed 13 wounded. Attack commenced 12 midnight and continued till daylight. The attack was made of a steadily rushing nature and very genuine. 40 S.R. joined. Casualties R.I. 1 killed 15 wounded.	(1)

B.A. Worthington Major
Commdg 1st Royal Irish Fusiliers.

19th Infantry Brigade.

2nd BATTALION

ROYAL WELCH FUSILIERS

NOVEMBER 1 9 1 4

WAR DIARY
or
INTELLIGENCE SUMMARY.
(Erase heading not required.)

Army Form C. 2118.

Instructions regarding War Diaries and Intelligence Summaries are contained in F.S. Regs., Part II. and the Staff Manual respectively. Title pages will be prepared in manuscript.

Hour, Date, Place	Summary of Events and Information	Remarks and references to Appendices
Nov. 2nd 1914 LA BOUTILLERIE FROMELLES	Slight attacks during the early morning, without disclosing themselves. Shelling, rather more advanced, has occurred just before dark. Casualties – R.J. Killed 4 wounded.	do 2/23
Nov 3rd 1914 "	Enemy quiet to our front. Enemy shelled a great deal in rear of our trenches. Reliefs – a Coy to 5th Reinforcements. 1st A Cooker 1-20 R.J. Garrison. Casualties R.J. 1 Killed 3 wounded.	do
Nov 3rd 1914 "	At Patrol from "B" Coy surprised the enemy digging and managed to bayonet four. Got Getting deeply into enemy trenches. Trenches were very heavily shelled during the day. Casualties 2nd Lt. Davies wounded. R.J. Killed 2, wounded 10.	do
Nov 4th 1914 "	Quiet night. Snow driving them back. During the day Casualties – 2 Opr R.A. Skippers Lt. Stretton wounded. R.J. 4 Killed. Stretcher b. 6 L. Reinforcements (a Shuffle or 37 men) arrived.	do
Nov 5th 1914 "	Incidentally quiet except for rifle fire & shelling in the evening. Casualties nil.	do
Nov 6th 1914 "	Heavy shelling of Trenches by our guns. Other firing in the morning, very quiet. Heavily shelled about 2.30 pm. Shot fired all night. Casualties R.J. 2 Killed 11 wounded.	do

Army Form C. 2118.

WAR DIARY
or
INTELLIGENCE SUMMARY.
(Erase heading not required.)

Instructions regarding War Diaries and Intelligence Summaries are contained in F.S. Regs., Part II. and the Staff Manual respectively. Title pages will be prepared in manuscript.

Hour, Date, Place	Summary of Events and Information	Remarks and references to Appendices
Nov 7th 1914. LA BOUTILLERIE	Stuck fast in the morning. Heavily shelled all day also at FRONTELLES night. Advances 4 killed 9 wounded	QD
Nov 8th 1914	Heavy shelling all day. Casualties 4 wounded. R of	QD 2/23rd
Nov 9th 1914	Quiet day. A small amount of firing at night. Queer sounds	QD
	heard at Prologue as he sounded two letters	
	Casualties R & ___ One wounded.	
Nov 10th 1914 "	Quiet day. A good deal of sniping about 4 am. Casualties R & ___ Two killed.	QD
Nov 11th 1914 "	Quiet day. 2nd Echelon got shelled & had to move back about 1000 yds. Casualties - nil -	QD
Nov 12th 1914 "	Quiet day. Wet and muddy. Casualties R & ___ 1 Killed, 1 Wounded.	QD
Nov 13th 1914 "	Quiet day. Again wet. ? Bus left us. Casualties R & ___ 1 Wounded.	QD
Nov 14th 1914 "	Quiet day. Wet relieved by 2/Scots Guards at 6 pm marched	QD
	to SAILLY & went into billets. Casualties R & ___ 2 Killed.	
Nov 15th 1914 SAILLY	In billets	QD
Nov 16th 1914 "	In billets	QD

Army Form C. 2118.

WAR DIARY
or
INTELLIGENCE SUMMARY.
(Erase heading not required.)

Instructions regarding War Diaries and Intelligence Summaries are contained in F.S. Regs., Part II. and the Staff Manual respectively. Title pages will be prepared in manuscript.

Hour, Date, Place	Summary of Events and Information	Remarks and references to Appendices
Nov. 19. 1914.	Marched off at 2 pm. Halting for tea at Armentières.	(1)
	Then proceeded to Houplines and took over the trenches	
	of B. Coy. Irish Guards and 3 & 4 Coy. Dublin Guards.	2/23
HOUPLINES		
Nov. 19th 1914. "	Very quiet, no casualties.	(1)
Nov. 19th 1914. "	Nothing doing. Heavy snow at front.	(1)
Nov. 20th 1914. "	Hard frost. All quiet	(1)
Nov. 21st 1914. "	Hard frost. All quiet	(1)
Nov. 22nd 1914. "	Hard frost. All quiet	(1)
Nov. 23rd 1914. "	Hard frost. All quiet	(1)
Nov. 24th 1914. "	"	(1)
Nov. 25 1914. "	Relieved at 5 pm. by Middlesex Regt. and went into	(1)
	Billets in Houplines.	
Nov. 26th 1914. "	In Billets - general clean up	(1)
Nov. 27 1914. "	Bn. Genl. Inspected the men in Billets	(1)
	at 10.30 a.m.	

Army Form C. 2118.

WAR DIARY
or
INTELLIGENCE SUMMARY.
(Erase heading not required.)

Instructions regarding War Diaries and Intelligence Summaries are contained in F. S. Regs., Part II. and the Staff Manual respectively. Title pages will be prepared in manuscript.

Hour, Date, Place	Summary of Events and Information	Remarks and references to Appendices

19th Brigade.

2nd BATTALION

ROYAL WELCH FUSILIERS

DECEMBER 1914

Army Form C. 2118.

WAR DIARY
or
INTELLIGENCE SUMMARY.
(Erase heading not required.)

Instructions regarding War Diaries and Intelligence Summaries are contained in F. S. Regs., Part II. and the Staff Manual respectively. Title pages will be prepared in manuscript.

Hour, Date, Place	Summary of Events and Information	Remarks and references to Appendices
December 1/1914. Houplines in Billets.		
2.1.1914.	One Company paraded to meet His Majesty The King. Coy. Sgt. Taylor was presented with D.C.M. by His Majesty.	C/o C/o
3.1914. b/ Frelinghien	Relieved the Camerounians in the trenches near Frelinghien at dark.	C/o
4th " "	Enemy amused themselves by aiming a kept on the walls of houses in rear of "A" Coy. until they cut a hole in the wall.	C/o
5th " "	Very wet all day – a great deal of house with parapets falling in, also trenches getting water logged. Enemy shelled HOUPLINES. One man killed.	C/o
6th " "	A good deal of falling in by enemy on HOUPLINES and by our own people on FRELINGHIEM. One man killed.	C/o
7th " "	Very wet – trenches all falling in.	C/o
8th " "	Heavy sniping all day – probably owing to enemy working in our trenches. Parapets all collapsing – one man wounded.	C/o

WAR DIARY
or
INTELLIGENCE SUMMARY.
(Erase heading not required.)

Army Form C. 2118.

Hour, Date, Place	Summary of Events and Information	Remarks and references to Appendices
Dec. 9th 1914 W. FRELINGHIEM.	Very wet - trenches waterlogged. Two men wounded. Middlesex Regt. & Argyll and Sutherland Highlanders attacked at 9.45 p.m. Nothing doing to our front.	
10th " "	Wet - very quiet all day.	C/o
11th " "	Wet.	C/o
12th " "	Wet. One man killed and one wounded.	C/o
13th " "	Very quiet. One man wounded - 95 Reinforcements & 1 missing man joined.	C/o
14th " "	Heavy shelling by our guns all along the line - a great amount of sniping and countersniping. Two men wounded.	C/o 2/23
15th " "	Heavy shelling by our guns - less sniping.	C/o
16th " "	Heavy sniping - countersniping our guns shelled enemy trenches.	C/o
17th " "	More shelling enemy all along the line - one man wounded.	C/o
18th " "	More sniping than usual - wet in the afternoon.	C/o
19th " "	Showery - enemy quiet at night. Heavy firing all day.	C/o

Army Form C. 2118.

WAR DIARY
or
INTELLIGENCE SUMMARY.
(Erase heading not required.)

Instructions regarding War Diaries and Intelligence Summaries are contained in F. S. Regs., Part II. and the Staff Manual respectively. Title pages will be prepared in manuscript.

Hour, Date, Place	Summary of Events and Information	Remarks and references to Appendices
Dec. 20th 1914 FRELINGHIEM	Parapets collapsed again - one man wounded.	
21st "	"B" Company flooded out - FRELINGHIEM shelled by the Division guns. Very wet in the afternoon.	
22nd "	Quiet day. Patrol found 6 our dead Germans & Rifles in front of "C" Company. 133rd Saxon Regt.	
23rd "	Slight sniping in morning - 2 our men wounded.	
24th "	Very quiet.	
25th "	Practically a truce all day. [Frost at night.] Both sides walked about on top of their trenches - allowed Germans to bury their dead. The following telegram was sent to His Majesty The King:- "All ranks 2nd Bn. Royal Welch Fusiliers wish their Colonel-in-Chief and Her Majesty a Merry Xmas and a Happy New-Year - commanding." The following reply was received :- "The Queen and I thank all ranks for their Xmas and	

Army Form C. 2118.

WAR DIARY
or
INTELLIGENCE SUMMARY.
(Erase heading not required.)

Hour, Date, Place	Summary of Events and Information	Remarks and references to Appendices
	(Continued)	
Dec. 25 1914 FRELINGHIEM.	New Years Greeting which we heartily reciprocate - George R.I. Colonel-in-Chief.	Qs
26th " h. ERQUINHIEM	Relieved at 5.p.m. by Durham Light Infantry. Went into billets near ERQUINHIEM.	Qs
27th " "	In billets. Very wet -	Qs
28th " "	In billets - Very wet - Blew a gale at night	Qo
29th " "	In billets	Qo
30th " "	In billets No 8795 Sergt T. Ledgton awarded D.C.M.	Qo
31st " "	In billets	Qo

O.C. Wilieiams. Major
Commdg 2 Bn Royal Welsh Fusiliers

Extract from letter of the late 2/Lieutenant M.S. Richardson,
2/Royal Welch Fusiliers, 19th Infantry Brigade, 6th Division,
III Corps, B.E.F.   25th December 1914, near Armentières.

- - - - - - - - - - - - - - - -

Then came a letter with the story of the Christmas Day truce; he writes "31/12/14. I will tell you of the extraordinary day we spent on Christmas Day. On Christmas Eve we had a sing-song with the men in the trenches, (this all applies to our Company - A). We put up a sheet of canvas, with a large 'Merry Christmas', and a portrait of the Kaiser painted on it, on the parapet. The next morning there was a thick fog, and when it lifted about 12, the Germans (Saxons) who were only 150 yards in front of us saw it, they began to shout across, and beckoning to our men to come half way and exchange gifts. They then came out of their trenches, and gave our men cigars and cigarettes, and 2 barrels of beer, in exchange for tins of bully beef. The situation was so absurd, that another officer of ours and myself went out, and met seven of their officers, and arranged that we should keep our men in our respective trenches, and that we should have an armistice till the next morning, when we would lower our Christmas card, and hostilities would continue. One of them presented me with the packet of cigarettes I sent you, and we gave them a plum pudding, and then we shook hands with them, and saluted each other, and returned to our respective trenches. Not a shot was fired all day, and the next morning we pulled our card down, and they put up one with 'thank you' on it".

19th Inf.Bde.
6th Div.

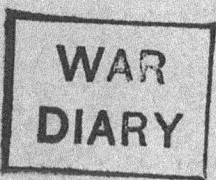

2nd BATTN. THE ROYAL WELCH FUSILIERS.

J A N U A R Y

1 9 1 5

INTELLIGENCE SUMMARY.

(Erase heading not required.)

Summaries are contained in F.S. Regs., Part II. and the Staff Manual respectively. Title pages will be prepared in manuscript.

Hour, Date, Place	Summary of Events and Information	Remarks and references to Appendices
1st Jan 1915 ERQUINGHEM	In Billets have received that Capt R.W. Phillips died of wounds received on November 3rd. Decr 29 1914 assault. Rumour received on November 3rd. Reinforcements 99 Other Ranks arrived.	do
2nd Jan 1915 CRIS-POT	Battalion moved to CRIS-POT about a mile away. In Brigade Reserve & therefore in Billets.	do
3rd Jan 1915 — " —	In Billets — Church Parade.	do
4th Jan 1915 — " —	In Billets.	do
5th Jan 1915 — " —	In Billets.	do
6th Jan 1915 — " —	In Billets.	do
7th Jan 1915 — " —	In Billets. Two officers rejoined & two reported asunder.	do
8th Jan 1915 — " —	2nd Lt. G.C.B. Bathurst & B. oy 2nd Lt. A.C. Attwater, C. oy.	do
9th Jan 1915 S.W. BOIS GRENIER	Relieved 1st Cameronians in trenches in front of BOIS GRENIER and went to trenches of 1st Batt N Reg. Relief thus: Trench very wet & much work to be done.	do
10th Jan 1915 — " —	Nothing to notice. Orders to make new parapet. Work done with difficulty. R.E. help. Very wet & much difficulty.	do

(Erase heading not required.)

...will be prepared in manuscript. Title pages ... respectively.

Hour, Date, Place	Summary of Events and Information	Remarks and references to Appendices
10th Jan 1915 BOIS GRENIER	Same as 9th. Casualties Rd. Pte Hare wounded BOIS GRENIER. Shelled.	Q.D.
11th Jan 1915 "	Nothing to note. One man killed one wounded.	Q.D.
12th Jan 1915 "	Party Battery shelled what they believed to be a searchlight in enemy trenches wherever it was it was knocked out. A little sniping.	Q.D.
13th Jan 1915 "	More sniping than usual. Enemy trenches shelled very well. Enemy shelled our Headquarters at about 11 am did some damage. Accounted for 9 snipers during the day - 7th Batt. took over trenches on our Right. Capt. Cowell & two men wounded.	Q.D.
14th Jan 1915 "	A good deal of sniping and countersniping during the day. Enemy shelled BOIS GRENIER.	Q.D.

2/23ᵃ

Hour, Date, Place	Summary of Events and Information	Remarks and references to Appendices
15ᵗʰ Janʸ 1915 BOIS GRENIER	Enemy shelled WATER FARM but did no damage:- machine guns located a trench content which they fired on.	do
16ᵗʰ Janʸ 1915	2ⁿᵈ L.N. Lancs & D. Co Kirkby reported themselves. Enemy shelled our day billets D. Coy located two Emmy's tob Guns and 2ⁿᵈ Battery managed to move them.	do
17ᵗʰ Janʸ 1915 "	2ⁿᵈ Lieut Owen moody & Thynne arr from Artists Rifles arrived. Quiet day [snow fell at night very cold.]	do
18ᵗʰ Janʸ 1915 "	Snow - SE all day - very quiet no shelling.	do
19ᵗʰ Janʸ 1915 GRIS-POT	Increase of Sniping - relieved by Cameronians went into billets at GRIS-POT.	do
20ᵗʰ Janʸ 1915 "	In billets. Wet	do
21ˢᵗ Janʸ 1915 "	In billets. Very wet	do
22ⁿᵈ Janʸ 1915 "	In billets - frost during night - fine day - Battʳ went out for Route march.	do

(Erase heading not required.)

Hour, Date, Place	Summary of Events and Information	Remarks and references to Appendices
23. Jan'y 1915 ARIS. POT.	In billets - fine day.	Q.O
24. Jan'y 1915 Bt BOIS GRENIER	Relieved Cameronians in trenches in front of BOIS GRENIER	Q.O
25. Jan'y 1915	Fine, work commenced in connecting up the line by breastwork. Lt Bemok + 50 others ranks one killed.	Q.O
26th Jan'y 1915	Heavy Bombardment of Enemy to our front by our Batteries followed by rapid fire from trenches - Result a certain amount of hostile parapet and wire blown down and a quantity of shells round two bodywaters. Casualties - One man killed two men wounded.	Q.O
27th Jan'y 1915	Quiet day Germans hardly fired a shot sharp frost at night.	Q.O
28th Jan'y 1915	Quiet day - attempted to snow - frost all day.	Q.O
29th Jan'y 1915	Enemy attempted to shell Salen Farm in the morning but without result. Relieved by Cameronians in evening & went into billets in ARIS. POT.	Q.O

Hour, Date, Place	Summary of Events and Information	Remarks and references to Appendices
30th Jan 1915 GRIS-POT	Parade.	do
31st Jan 1915	Church Parade. Battn ordered to arms at 9 am.	do

D.M. Williams Major
Comdg. 2nd Bn Ry. Welch Fus.

19th Inf.Bde.
6th Div.

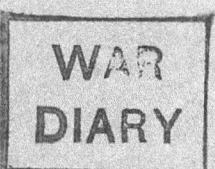

2nd BATTN. THE ROYAL WELCH FUSILIERS.

F E B R U A R Y

1 9 1 5

INTELLIGENCE SUMMARY.

(Erase heading not required.)

Instructions regarding War Diaries and Intelligence Summaries are contained in F.S. Regs., Part II. and the Staff Manual respectively. Title pages will be prepared in manuscript.

Hour, Date, Place	Summary of Events and Information	Remarks and references to Appendices
1st February 1915 BOIS-GRENIER	In billets – Good hard and [Brigadier General] inspected the billets in the morning. Lieut. C. Worthy rejoined with 50 Reinforcements &c. one man wounded.	do
2nd " "	In billets – Stood to arms 7 am.	do
3rd " "		do
4th " BOIS GRENIER	Relieved Camerons in trenches in the evening. A certain amount of shelling during the day – at 7 pm. enemy's guns opened and about 9.10 pm enemy opened rapid fire, our guns replied. Two french mortars were turned on to us. One died down at about 9.40. from quiet night. Two killed six wounded.	do
5th " "	Quiet day – one man wounded.	do
6th " "	Quiet day, annoyed by Searchlight a good deal during the night.	do
7th " "	Increase of sniping.	do

7/2/3rd

and the Staff Manual respectively. Title pages will be prepared in manuscript.

(Erase heading not required.)

Hour, Date, Place	Summary of Events and Information	Remarks and references to Appendices
8 February 1915 CRIS-POT	Relieved by Camerons in the evening went into Billets in CRIS-POT.	do
9 "	On Billets	do
10 "	On Billets	do
11 "	On Billets	do
12 "	On Billets] one man wounded with working party - very wet	do
13 "		do
" Nr BOIS GRENIER	Relieved Camerons and in trenches in the evening very wet	
14 "	Quiet day - heavy rain.	do
15 "	Very wet - one man wounded - quiet day.	do
16 "	Fine - Increase of sniping. Enemy fired at our aeroplane but were soon silenced by their trenches being shelled by our guns.	do
17 "	A lot of sniping - very wet - one man wounded.	do

(9 29 6) W 2794 100,000 5/14 H W V Forms/C. 2118/11

INTELLIGENCE SUMMARY.

(Erase heading not required.)

Summaries are contained in F. S. Regs., Part II. and the Staff Manual respectively. Title pages will be prepared in manuscript.

Hour, Date, Place	Summary of Events and Information	Remarks and references to Appendices
18th February 1915 O.R.'s P.O.T.	A lot of sniping - nothing on our right. One man wounded. Relieved Sir Bermereins at 8 p.m.	2/0
19th "	In Billets - one shell dropped in during afternoon.	2/0
20th "	In Billets - 2nd Lieut F. S. Craig and 29 N.C.O's & men mostly wounded & sick reported their arrival.	2/0
21st "	In Billets	2/0
22nd "	In Billets	2/0
23rd " W. BOISGRENIER	Relieved Carmereins in trenches at 7.8 p.m.	2/0
24th "	Quiet day - snowstorm. Lieut C.O.R.E. inspected "a" & "B" Co'ys Trenches.	2/0
25th "	Quiet day fine one man wounded.	2/0
26th "	Thick fog till noon - fine day. Brigadier General went round "C" & "D" Co'ys Trenches.	2/0

INTELLIGENCE SUMMARY.

(Erase heading not required.)

Summaries are contained in F.S. Regs., Part II. and the Staff Manual respectively. Title pages will be prepared in manuscript.

Hour, Date, Place	Summary of Events and Information	Remarks and references to Appendices
the 20th February 1915 N. BOIS GRENIER	Enemy fired rifle grenades without result except that we shelled their trenches in return.	do
28th — GRIS-POT.	Enemy shelled BOIS GRENIER and farms in rear of our line most of the day - one man killed. Relieved by Cameronians at 8 p.m. To billets.	do

Alongh Captain
Comdg. 2nd Bn Roy Welch Fus:

Month K.L.W.
joined 2 + 79.

2/23 M

19th Inf.Bde.
6th Div.

2nd BATTN. THE ROYAL WELCH FUSILIERS.

M A R C H

1 9 1 5

INTELLIGENCE SUMMARY.

(Erase heading not required.)

Instructions regarding War Diaries and Intelligence Summaries are contained in F. S. Regs., Part II. and the Staff Manual respectively. Title pages will be prepared in manuscript.

Hour, Date, Place	Summary of Events and Information	Remarks and references to Appendices
1st March 1915 GRIS-POT.	In billets – a few shells dropped rather close in the afternoon.	do
2nd " "	In billets.	do
3rd " "	In billets.	do
4th " "	In billets.	do
5th " N. BOIS GRENIER	Relieved Cameronians in trenches at 7 p.m.	do
6th " "	Very wet – one man wounded.	do
7th " "	Wet – quiet day.	do
8th " "	Showed in morning – quiet day – froot at night	do
9th " "	Fine – Enemys trenches shelled slightly. Two men wounded on patrol.	do
10th " GRIS-POT.	Enemys trenches bombarded, they did not make much reply. One man killed one wounded. Relieved by Cameronians at 7 p.m.	do
11th " "	In billets. No one allowed out of billets owing to bombardment of enemy in front of our line.	do

INTELLIGENCE SUMMARY.

(Erase heading not required.)

Summaries are contained in F. S. Regs., Part II. and the Staff Manual respectively. Title pages will be prepared in manuscript.

Hour, Date, Place	Summary of Events and Information	Remarks and references to Appendices
12th March 15. CRIS-POT.	In Billets – Confined to Billets.	do
13th " L'ARMEÉ	In Billets – took over Billets of Middlesex Regt. at L'ARMEÉ in the evening – 25 Reinforcements etc arrived.	do
14th " "	In Billets.	do
15th " (") LA YESÉE	Relieved Argyll & Sutherland Highlanders in trenches opposite LA YESÉE at 6. p.m. A good deal of sniping – Two killed one wounded.	do
16th " "	Heavy sniping all day & night shelled enemy's trenches which stopped them a bit.	do
17th " "	A good deal of sniping both by day & night. One wounded 2nd Lieut Williams & 42 Reinforcements etc arrived.	do
18th " "	Shelled enemy's trenches in early morning – much less sniping both by day & night	do
19th " "	Quiet day – very little sniping – slight snow.	do

INTELLIGENCE SUMMARY.
(Erase heading not required.)

Hour, Date, Place	Summary of Events and Information	Remarks and references to Appendices
20th March 1915 W LA YESÉE	Increase of sniping - machine guns enfiladed "C" & "D" Coys. 2nd Scottish Borderers & one man killed. Two wounded. Set Goderick awarded D.C.M. for gallant conduct on patrol on night 12th inst.	Do
21st — L'ARMÉE.	Quiet day - relieved by Middlesex Regt at 8 p.m. went into billets at L'ARMÉE.	Do
22nd — "	In billets. "A" & "B" Coys moved into fresh billets. "C" & "D" Coys moved into G RIS POT at 9 p.m.	Do 1/2³
23rd — GRIS-POT.	Billets at GRIS POT at 9 p.m. GRIS-POT Billets shelled in the afternoon - "C" & "D" and Headquarters moved into GRIS-POT Billets at 9 p.m. Lieut. R.R. Smollyn awarded The Military Cross for gallant work on patrol on night of 12th inst.	Do
24th — "	In billets - IS et.	Do
25th — "	In billets	Do
26th — W LA YESÉE	Relieved Middlesex Regt. in trenches at about 8 p.m. One man wounded.	Do

INTELLIGENCE SUMMARY.

(Erase heading not required.)

Hour, Date, Place	Summary of Events and Information	Remarks and references to Appendices
27th March 1916 Nr LA VESÉE	Enemy much quieter. Believed to be Saxons. Several aeroplanes over during day – very fine & cold.	Q.o
28th "	Cpt. A.C.O. Whodon & 2 men wounded out of patrol in early morning – Two men wounded on wiring party – Enemy's machine Gun active during the night.	Q.o
29th "	Quiet day – 4 shells dropped in front of "C" Coy's parapet at about 10.30 p.m. 2 men wounded.	Q.o
30th "	Enemy shelled "A" & "B" Coy's trenches – no damage was done. One man wounded. Capt. Stockwell left to join 7th Bn.	Q.o
31st " GRIS-POT.	Quiet day – Relieved by Middlesex Regt. & at 8 p.m.	Q.o

1st April 1915.

O.B.S.L. Williams, Major
Comdg. 2nd Bn. Roy. Welsh Fus.

19th Inf.Bde.
6th Div.

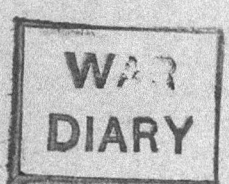

2nd BATTN. THE ROYAL WELCH FUSILIERS.

A P R I L

1 9 1 5

INTELLIGENCE SUMMARY.

(Erase heading not required.)

Hour, Date, Place	Summary of Events and Information	Remarks and references to Appendices
1st April 1915. GRIS-POT.	In billets - Enemy shelled cross roads & L'ARMÉE cross roads.	Do
2nd " "	In billets - Church Service	Do
3rd " "	In billets	Do 2/23
4th " W. BOIS GRENIER.	In billets - Church Service - Relieved Argyll and Sutherland Highlanders in trenches in front of BOIS GRENIER at about 8 p.m. A good deal of sniping at night.	Do
5th " "	Rain all day. Enemy sniped heavily at dawn. 2nd Lt. Wagner Roy. Warwicks reported his arrival. Capt. Malby wounded.	Do
6th " "	Colonel of Kitcheners Army attached for 24 hours. 2nd Lt. Gee 7th Roy. Fus. and 8 men reported their arrival.	Do
7th " "	Very quiet - [Brigadier went round trenches at night - one man wounded]	Do

INTELLIGENCE SUMMARY.

(Erase heading not required.)

and the Staff Manual respectively. Title pages will be prepared in manuscript.

Hour, Date, Place		Summary of Events and Information	Remarks and references to Appendices
9th April 1915	BOIS GRENIER	Rain and sleet. Quiet day.	Do
10th	GRIS POT.	Lieut Col S. Richardson and two men wounded by rifle grenade. Trenches shelled at about 5 p.m. Relieved by Cameronians at 8 p.m. To billets behind	Do
11th		GRIS POT. In Billets.	Do
12th		In Billets.	Do
13th		In Billets.	Do
14th		In Billets. 2nd Lieut St. H. Cooke Unattached List. Indian Army reported his arrival.	Do
15th	W. BOIS GRENIER	In Billets. Relieved Cameronians in the trenches at about 8 p.m.	Do
16th		Enemy fired a good deal in the early morning and sent some hand grenades over. Also shelled Left of "C" Coy. One man wounded.	Do
17th		Fine – very quiet – one man wounded.	Do

INTELLIGENCE SUMMARY.

(Erase heading not required.)

Hour, Date, Place	Summary of Events and Information	Remarks and references to Appendices
18th April 1915 Bois Grenier	Fine – a little more sniping in the evening – Enemy fired about 12 shells at Flamendrie Farm at night no damage.	Q
19th "	General Gordon visited the trenches in the afternoon. A few shells fired near Flamendrie early in the night.	Q 2/23
20th " Gris Pot	Four Bursts of Shrapnel fired at "D" & "D" Coms – ranies during the day no damage done – Relieved by Cameronians at about 9 p.m. to billets – One man wounded. One man wounded.	Q
21st "	In Billets.	Q
22nd "	In Billets – one man wounded working on communication trench.	Q
23rd "	In Billets.	Q
24th "	Artillery bombarded enemy's lines – Confined to Billets.	Q

INTELLIGENCE SUMMARY.

(Erase heading not required.)

Hour, Date, Place	Summary of Events and Information	Remarks and references to Appendices
25th April 1915. BOIS GRENIER	Relieved Cameronians in trenches at about 8:30.p.m. - Germans very noisy - one man wounded - 25 Reinforcements arrived.	do
26th "	Several rifle grenades fired at "a" Coy. during the afternoon. 2/Lieut. Goldsmith from Coldstreamers reported his arrival. Enemy fired two Salvoes at 8:30.p.m. and 11:30.p.m. at Flamengrie Farm and Communication trench - One man killed.	do
27th "	Enemy fired one Salvoe on TOUQUET - Water Farm road - Enemy very active on appearance of aeroplanes - 1 man killed 1 wounded - 36 Reinforcements arrived.	do
28th "	Heavy sniping at dawn - Enemy fired 3 Salvoes on trenches between 8.p.m. and 11.p.m. - one man slightly wounded.	do

Hour, Date, Place	Summary of Events and Information	Remarks and references to Appendices
29. April 1915. N. BOIS GRENIER	Enemy fired one Salvoe on trenches at about 11.0 a.m. - another at 2.30 p.m. and another at 9.20 p.m. on wire party - the latter killed two and wounded three men.	as
30th. GRIS POT.	Quiet day - relieved by Cameronians at 8.30 p.m. to Riddels. One man wounded	as

D.R. Wilkinson
Major
Comdg 2nd Roy Welch Fus

1. May 1915.

19th Inf.Bde.
6th Div.

Battn. with Bd
joined 27th Di
31.5.15.

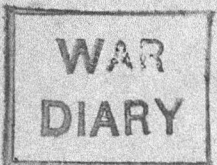

2nd BATTN. THE ROYAL WELCH FUSILIERS.

M A Y

1 9 1 5

Hour, Date, Place	Summary of Events and Information	Remarks and references to Appendices
1st May 1915. CRIS P.O.T.	In billets - Lieut Eyre reported his arrival	do
2nd " "	In billets - cold & wet 2/Lt K.L. Hutchings	do
	Kings reported his arrival	
3rd " "	In billets.	do
4th " "	In billets - wet afternoon.	do
5th " BOIS GRENIER.	Relieved Connaughts in trenches at about 9 p.m.	do
6th " "	Enemy fired a few Salvoes during the day mostly in	do
	rear of Flamengrie	
7th " "	Enemy's wire bombarded at 6.30 p.m. and various	do
	other orders given out shortly after the bombardment	
	all orders were cancelled - Enemy were not	
	able to mend their wire.	
8th " "	Very quiet day - Battery fired star shell at 10 p.m.	do
	and set something on fire in rear of German	
	trenches which burned all night	
	Casualty one wounded.	

(Erase heading not required.)

will be prepared in manuscript.

Hour, Date, Place	Summary of Events and Information	Remarks and references to Appendices
9 Nov 1915. W. BOIS GRENIER.	Bombarded enemys trenches and ground at rear from 4.30 a.m. to 5.10 a.m. Heavy firing on our right opposite FROMELLES.	do
	Enemy reply feeble - on the whole exceptionally quiet. At about 9.30 p.m. to 11 p.m. a great deal of transport was heard moving South. Sn. killed one wounded.	do
10th — CRIS POT.	Enemy shelled in rear of 'A' & 'B' Coy's trenches between 1.30 a.m. & 2.15 a.m. also communication trench at 9.30 a.m. — Relieved by Devonshires about 8.30 p.m. 2 Lieut Caldwell sick to England. In Billets.	do
11th — " —		do
12th — " —	In Billets - Bishop of Pretoria spoke to men at L'ARMEE at 3 p.m. In Billets.	do
13th — " —	In Billets.	do
14th — " —	West Riding Division bombarded enemys to their front for 10 minutes at 1 a.m. — In Billets.	do

(Erase heading not required.)

Hour, Date, Place	Summary of Events and Information	Remarks and references to Appendices
15 May 1915 Bois Grenier 4h	Further bombardment by West Riding Division at 5 a.m. and 9 a.m. Relieved Cameronians in the trenches at about 9 p.m.	do
16th " 1h	Bombardment of enemy's wire opposite Middlesex Regt at 11:15 a.m. and 8 p.m. Very quiet to our front. One man killed.	do
17th " 4h	Very quiet all day. A Zeppelin sighted at 4 + 5 a.m. about 10 m to the N flying towards East. Between 11 p.m. + midnight - Artillery + machine gun fire was directed on farms + trenches in rear of German lines - which caused attack signals + several flares to be sent up	do
18th " "	Very quiet all day - wet.	do
19th " "	Quiet day - wet - 11 officers K.O.S.B's Kitcheners Army attached for 24 hours. One man wounded.	do
20th " "	Increase of sniping at daylight also several shells + rifle grenades sent over - Gradually change of shorts to our front - Relieved by Cameronians at about 9 p.m. 1 man killed. 4 wounded (1 died of wounds)	do

Hour, Date, Place	Summary of Events and Information	Remarks and references to Appendices
21. May 1915. CRISPOT.	In Billets.	do
22nd " "	In Billets – Some shells dropped near men playing football in the afternoon & in the evening one shell hit our Headquarters severely wounding one man who died during the night.	do
23rd " "	In Billets.	do
24th " "	In Billets. Trenches in front of BRIDOUX at 6 p.m. – a Brigade of West Riding Division took upon advanced line with two companies astride BRIDOUX road. Bombardment carried on at intervals throughout the night	do
25th " "	In Billets – should have gone into trenches at night but this was cancelled.	do
26th " "	In Billets – relieved Cameronians in trenches at about 9 p.m. one man wounded.	do

(Erase heading not required.)

Hour, Date, Place	Summary of Events and Information	Remarks and references to Appendices
27th May 1915 W. BOIS GRENIER	Quiet day. Trenches on our right were shelled at intervals during the day — a few shells fell well behind our trenches doing no damage — on our right we dug 30 yards of new trench to cover our right flank. Lieut J & J Evans & one man reported their arrival.	Qo
28th —	Two shells dropped in 'C' Coy's trench at about 1pm. 36th Battery took over from 92nd in support of us — Two men wounded.	Qo
29th —	A few shells fired at intervals during the day — one man killed.	Qo
30th —	Very quiet all day. A lot of firing to the N. during the night.	Qo
31st —	Enemy fired 2 shells near 'A' Company about 5 am. to 5.30 am No damage was done. Relieved by Cameronians at about 9 pm. Attached to 27th Division =	Qo

D.A. Stevenson
Major
Comdg. 2nd Bn. Roy. Welch Fus.

1st June 1915.

Cs. mark K.C.W.9

27TH DIVISION
19TH INFY BDE

2ND BN ROY. WELCH FUS.
JUN - JLY 1915

27TH DIVISION
19TH INFY BDE

19th Infantry Brigade.

27th Division.

(Battn. with Bde. left 6th
Division on 31.5.15)

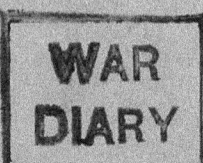

2nd BATTN. THE ROYAL WELCH FUSILIERS.

J U N E

1 9 1 5

WAR DIARY
or
INTELLIGENCE SUMMARY.
(Erase heading not required.)

Instructions regarding War Diaries and Intelligence Summaries are contained in F. S. Regs., Part II. and the Staff Manual respectively. Title pages will be prepared in manuscript.

Hour, Date, Place	Summary of Events and Information	Remarks and references to Appendices
1st June 1915. GRIS-POT.	In Billets.	Qo
2nd " W. LA YESEE.	In Billets - relieved Argyll & Sutherland Highlanders on left Section - Middlesex on our left in RUE DU BOIS trenches - A good deal of sniping during the night.	Qo
3rd " — "	Enemy shelled our line during the day also supports and 2nd line but no damage was done - Bomb voices were heard in the German trenches during the night.	Qo
4th " — "	A good deal of shelling all day - Parapet badly blown in in "B" Company - Sgt Mackey and a patrol of 3 men successfully bombed a German patrol - Two men wounded.	Qo
5th " — "	A good deal of sniping and shelling - Billet farm was shelled in the evening causing 4 casualties one being killed - Reserve platoon was moved further back. LA YESEE. Casualties: 1 killed 4 wounded.	Qo

INTELLIGENCE SUMMARY.

(Erase heading not required.)

Instructions regarding War Diaries and Intelligence Summaries are contained in F.S. Regs., Part II. and the Staff Manual respectively. Title pages will be prepared in manuscript.

Hour, Date, Place	Summary of Events and Information	Remarks and references to Appendices
6th June 1915. LA VESÉE.	Quiet all day - Burnt Farm and Communication Trench shelled about 8.15. p.m.	20
7th " "	We turned our machine guns on a working party at 12.35 a.m. and gave them some more at about 1 a.m. Support trench heavily shelled by big guns between 5.45 a.m. and 6.45 p.m. (Enemy's working parties fired on during the night. Two men wounded.	20
8th " "	Two shells very near Headquarters in the afternoon. Quiet day on the whole - relieved by Middlesex Regt. in the evening - One man wounded.	20
9th " GRIS-POT.	In Billets - Lieut Murphy sick.	20
10th " "	In Billets - relieved Argyll & Sutherland Highlanders in the trenches on Right of Line at 9.30 p.m., 1 man missing.	20
11th " Bt BOIS GRENIER.	Some shelling but no damage done - Snipers more active than usual - One man wounded.	20

INTELLIGENCE SUMMARY.

(Erase heading not required.)

Hour, Date, Place	Summary of Events and Information	Remarks and references to Appendices
12th June 1915 N. BOIS GRENIER	Snipers very active in front of "C" Coy – N°3 Farm was shelled by our Battery who drove three men out of the Farm – Main Communication trench shelled at about 6 p.m. One man wounded.	do
13th " "	Snipers active – "B" Coys trenches shelled in the evening. Casualties 2 killed one wounded.	do
14th " "	BOIS GRENIER heavily shelled in the afternoon – Two shells burst in "D" Coy: at 6.15 p.m. and about one in "C" Coy at 11.30.p.m. Casualties 4 men wounded.	do
15th " "	Quiet day on the whole. Lt. Moshyn went out with an officer sent down by Corps to try to discover what troops were in front of us – Capt J. Guthrie gazetted to Regiment as Captain dated February 1st	do
16th " "	Quiet all day until 6.30 p.m. when B & "D" Coys trenches were shelled – Relieved by Middlesex Regiment at 9.30.p.m. – 5 men wounded.	do

INTELLIGENCE SUMMARY.

(Erase heading not required.)

Hour, Date, Place	Summary of Events and Information	Remarks and references to Appendices
17 June 1915 CRIS-POT.	In billets.	do
18th "	2nd billets relieved Argylls & Sutherland Highlanders in RUE DU BOIS trenches at 9.30 pm. Lt Williams to hospital.	do
19th RUE DU BOIS	A good deal of shelling all day - mostly in rear of the trenches - one man injured by rifle flowing back.	do
20th "	Enemy open fire in the morning - four killed and four wounded by rifle grenades.	do
21st "	Quiet day on the whole - one man wounded.	do
22nd "	Quiet day - A great deal of cheering in the German trenches at night.	do
23rd "	Quiet day - Enemy new trench in front of house in "B" Coy. Nothing much fired on - no casualties. Lieut J. M. J. Hearns to J. Sam.	do
24th "	One Howitzer shelled Salient. Enemy retaliated with Trench mortars & rifle grenades. Relieved by Argylls & Sutherland Highlanders at about 10.30 p.m. 2nd Lieut Higgilson & Craig wounded by rifle grenade. One Jenkins man killed & one wounded by rifle grenade.	do

INTELLIGENCE SUMMARY.

(Erase heading not required.)

Hour, Date, Place	Summary of Events and Information	Remarks and references to Appendices
25th June 1915. CRIS-POT.	In billets. Despatches London Gazette 22nd mentioned Major O. De C. Williams — Battle O. S. Owen A. C. Samson & J. A. Childe-Freeman. also Lieut F. J. Inskyn. Honours London Gazette 23rd instant. Major O. De C. Williams to be Brevet Lt Col. Captain O. S. Owens D.S.O. Capt. A. C. Samson & Ja. Childe-Freeman — military Cross. 2nd Lieut Rugg M.C. & 50 other ranks reinforcements arrived.	do
26th " " —	In billets.	do
27th " " —	In billets.	do
28th " " —	In billets. One man killed and one wounded by shell on road.	do
29th " " —	In billets. relieved Cameronians in trenches at about 9.30 p.m. heavy rain — took over new line extending up to and including Bridoux road on right and gave up Sub Sec: 53 in front of Flamengrie Farm.	do

INTELLIGENCE SUMMARY.

(Erase heading not required.)

Instructions regarding War Diaries and Intelligence Summaries are contained in F. S. Regs., Part II. and the Staff Manual respectively. Title pages will be prepared in manuscript.

Hour, Date, Place	Summary of Events and Information	Remarks and references to Appendices
30th June 1915 Bois Grenier	Set all day - Enemy active with rifle grenades one man killed 3 wounded. O 52 Battery shelled Salient opposite Sub Sec 51 at 8.30 p.m.	00

J D Williams
Lieut Colonel
Comdg 2nd Bn. Roy. Welch Fusiliers

1st July 1915

19th Infantry Brigade.

27th Division.

(Battn. with Bde. joined
2nd Division on 19.8.15)

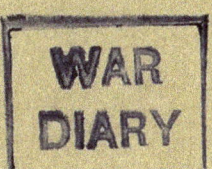

2nd BATTN. THE ROYAL WELCH FUSILIERS.

J U L Y

1 9 1 5

INTELLIGENCE SUMMARY.

(Erase heading not required.)

Instructions regarding War Diaries and Intelligence Summaries are contained in F. S. Regs., Part II. and the Staff Manual respectively. Title pages will be prepared in manuscript.

Hour, Date, Place	Summary of Events and Information	Remarks and references to Appendices
1st July 1915 BOIS GRENIER	Enemy's trenches opposite Sub Sect^{rs} 49 & 50 bombarded by our Field Guns & Howitzers at 11 a.m. Enemy replied with about 35 shells – no damage. "A" Company gave up Sub Sect^r 49 and moved back into Sub Sect^r 53.	QO
2nd " "	Hostile aeroplane passed over the line at 6.30 p.m. and was fired on – Enemy retaliated by firing rifle Grenades & shelling trenches. One man wounded	QO
3rd " "	Quiet day – Heavy sniping at night. Brigades on our right sent up Coloured Rockets.	QO
4th " "	Quiet day – very hot, relieved by Cameronians at 10 p.m. – to Billets.	QO
5th " GRIS-POT.	In Billets.	QO
6th " "	In Billets – Heavy thunderstorm during the night	QO
7th " "	In Billets – a good deal of rain during the day.	QO
8th " "	In Billets – GRIS-POT shelled at 4.15 p.m. Argyll & Sutherland Highlanders Hut hit.	QO

INTELLIGENCE SUMMARY.

(Erase heading not required.)

Instructions regarding War Diaries and Intelligence Summaries are contained in F.S. Regs., Part II. and the Staff Manual respectively. Title pages will be prepared in manuscript.

Hour, Date, Place	Summary of Events and Information	Remarks and references to Appendices
9th July 1915. GRIS-POT.	Relieved Cameronians in the trenches at 10 p.m. a bit of sniping during the night	Qo
10th " W BOIS GRENIER	2nd Lt Lee & 2nd Lt Bon Zui and one man killed in the early morning – very heavy sniping between 1 a.m. and 2 a.m. Enemy considerably more active all day	Qo
11th " "	Snipers active all day, one man killed on listening post in early morning – 3 men killed and 2 injured tampering with one unexploded fuze.	Qo
12th " "	A/53 fired Salvo on Salient opposite "C" Coy. at 2 a.m. Enemy considerably quieter all day.	Qo
13th " "	Enemy shelled moat farm at about 6 p.m. no damage was done – One man killed in early morning.	Qo
14th " "	Snipers very active at dawn – Relieved by Cameronians at about 10 p.m. Two men wounded.	Qo
15th " GRIS-POT.	In Billets. Twenty reinforcements arrived.	Qo
16th " "	In Billets. One man wounded while on trench fatigue.	Qo

INTELLIGENCE SUMMARY.

(Erase heading not required.)

Hour, Date, Place	Summary of Events and Information	Remarks and references to Appendices
17 July 1915. CRIS-POT.	In billets	do
18th " "	In billets.	do
19th " "	Battalion moved to billets near STEENWERCK - Seven men fell out.	do
20th " W. STEENWERCK.	In billets.	do
21st " "	In billets	do
22nd " "	In billets. 2nd Lt. H.P. Tiley 3rd East Surrey Regt. reported his arrival.	do
23rd " "	Moved into trenches at FAUQUISSART, taking them over from 1/4th Loyal Royal Lancaster Regt. Lieut. Lyle to Hospital sick.	do
24th " FAUQUISSART.	Enemy very quiet. Two patrols went out. enemy wire very strong.	do
25th " "	Quiet day - Enemy fired on B Coys party cutting grass in front killing one man at about 10.16 p.m.	do

INTELLIGENCE SUMMARY.

(Erase heading not required.)

Instructions regarding War Diaries and Intelligence Summaries are contained in F. S. Regs., Part II. and the Staff Manual respectively. Title pages will be prepared in manuscript.

Hour, Date, Place	Summary of Events and Information	Remarks and references to Appendices
26th July 1915 FAUQUISSART.	"A" Company fired on enemy's working party early in morning also D Company during the night. Both were dispersed. Two men wounded slightly by splinters	1
27th "	Quiet day. Shelled and opened fire on enemy working parties all along our line at 11.30 p.m. They retaliated with hand mortars, rifle grenades and rifle fire, the latter well over our trenches. Two men wounded	2
28th "	Enemy shelled right of our line between trenches and Rue TILLELOY doing no damage. One man wounded.	3
29th "	Relieved by 5th Scottish Rifles at about 9 p.m. went into billets in LAVENTIE.	4
30th " LAVENTIE. In Billets.		5

INTELLIGENCE SUMMARY.

(Erase heading not required.)

Hour, Date, Place	Summary of Events and Information	Remarks and references to Appendices
31 July 1915. LAVENTIE.	2nd Battn. "B", "C" & "D" Companies and Machine Guns moved up into Subsidiary Line in evening and took over posts from Coversations. "A" Company and Battalion Headquarters remained in LAVENTIE. 2nd Lieut. Jas. Soames reported his arrival.	(D)

Bn W. Mulholland Lieut. Colonel
Comdg 2nd Bn. Roy. Welsh Fusiliers

1st August 1915.

2ND DIVISION
19TH INFY BDE

2ND BATTALION
ROYAL WELCH FUSILIERS
AUG - NOV 1915

(To 33 DIV 19 BDE)

19th Infantry Brigade.

2nd Division.

(Battn. with Bde left 27th Div. on 19.8.15)

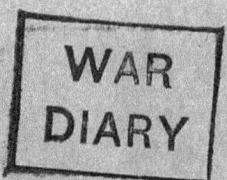

2nd BATTN. THE ROYAL WELCH FUSILIERS.

A U G U S T

1 9 1 5

Army Form C. 2118.

WAR DIARY
or
INTELLIGENCE SUMMARY.
(Erase heading not required.)

Instructions regarding War Diaries and Intelligence Summaries are contained in F. S. Regs., Part II. and the Staff Manual respectively. Title pages will be prepared in manuscript.

Hour, Date, Place	Summary of Events and Information	Remarks and references to Appendices
1 August 1915 LAVENTIE.	"C" Coy. moved into billets in Eastern portion of LAVENTIE. "B" Coy. moved back from Subsidiary Line into billets in same quarter. 20 Reinforcements arrived.	Q.o
2nd " "	In Billets — some rain.	Q.o
3rd " "	In Billets.	Q.o
4th " "	Relieved Middlesex Regt. in trenches in front of RUE TILLELOY about 9 p.m. very quiet night	Q.o
5th W. RUE TILLELOY.	Very heavy firing at one of our aeroplanes at 12.30 which was stopped by our batteries shelling enemy trenches. Enemy fired a few rifle grenades at 4.30 p.m. which did no damage. 25 Reinforcements arrived.	Q.o
6th " "	One man killed and one wounded during the early morning. Capt. Trench and Lieut. Coyle rejoined from Hospital. One man wounded on sentry during night.	Q.o

WAR DIARY or INTELLIGENCE SUMMARY

Army Form C. 2118.

Hour, Date, Place	Summary of Events and Information	Remarks and references to Appendices
7th August 1915. RUE TILLELOY.	Enemy retaliated to our artillery fire with a few minutes during the afternoon we replied with rifle grenades and also got our suffocating Batteries to fire. We obtained a direct hit on mortar position. Lieut Crosby slightly wounded in arm on patrol. Also one man & 2 men of 11th Rifle Brigade attached.	do
8th " "	Quiet day – Enemy opened burst of fire on our working parties during first part of the night. One man wounded.	do
9th " "	Quiet day – Machine Gun located – Bgd fired a salvo at 8.30 pm on supposed position which appeared to have the desired effect as it did not open fire again – one man wounded.	do
10th " "	Very misty in the morning – Relieved by Middlesex Regt at 9 p.m. to Billets in LAVENTIE.	do

WAR DIARY
or
INTELLIGENCE SUMMARY.
(Erase heading not required.)

Army Form C. 2118.

Instructions regarding War Diaries and Intelligence Summaries are contained in F. S. Regs., Part II. and the Staff Manual respectively. Title pages will be prepared in manuscript.

Hour, Date, Place	Summary of Events and Information	Remarks and references to Appendices
11th August 1915. LAVENTIE.	In Billets.	do
12th " "	In Billets – 2nd Lieut. Soames went to Royal Flying Corps on probation.	do
13th " "	In Billets.	do
14th " "	In Billets.	do
15th " "	Battalion handed over billets ac. to 11th R.B. at 6 p.m. and moved off at 8 p.m. to new billets near DOULIEU – VIEUX BERQUIN.	do
16th " DOULIEU – VIEUX BERQUIN.	In Billets.	do
17th " "	In Billets.	do
18th " "	Battalion marched to Forêt de Nieppe – had dinners and marched back to Billets.	do
19th " BETHUNE.	4th Infantry Brigade marched to BETHUNE via MERVILLE to join 2nd Division, marched past Lord Kitchener en route – To Billets in BETHUNE. Brigade in Corps reserve.	do

Army Form C. 2118.

WAR DIARY
or
INTELLIGENCE SUMMARY.
(Erase heading not required.)

Instructions regarding War Diaries and Intelligence Summaries are contained in F. S. Regs., Part II. and the Staff Manual respectively. Title pages will be prepared in manuscript.

Hour, Date, Place	Summary of Events and Information	Remarks and references to Appendices
20th August 1915. BETHUNE.	In billets – Battalion on duty from 4 p.m. until 4 p.m. 21st. 2nd Lieut. Soames to Royal Flying Corps.	Q0
21st. "	In billets – M.O.C. 2nd Division inspected the Battalion at 3.15 p.m.	Q0
22nd. "	In billets – Church Parade in Theatre at 9.30 a.m. The General Officer Commanding 2nd Division attended. Battalion marched past after service.	Q0
23rd "	In billets – one officer and 4 n.c. officers from each Company went into trenches in front of Cuinchy.	Q0
24th " CUINCHY.	Battalion took over CUINCHY trenches from Royal Berkshire Regiment at 3 p.m. Enemy comparatively quiet.	Q0
25 "	Enemy shelled Railway Bridge in rear of Left Company at 8.30 a.m. – Slight amount of shelling and counter shelling during the day – Enemy shelled Harley Street between 5 and 6 p.m. Our trench mortars dispersed	Q0

WAR DIARY
or
INTELLIGENCE SUMMARY.
(Erase heading not required.)

Army Form C. 2118.

Hour, Date, Place	Summary of Events and Information	Remarks and references to Appendices
25 August 1915, CUINCHY (continued)	an enemy working party in front of Bunker Company. Our working parties heavily sniped at night — Casualties one killed and one wounded.	C20
26 August 1915, CUINCHY.	Enemy shelled CUINCHY in the morning — our working party on Sapheard No. 15 Crater heavily bombed at about 10.30 p.m. — we replied with trench mortars and rifle grenades which caused enemy to open with their minenwerfer eventually silenced by our Howitzers.	C20
— " —	Quiet morning — relieved by Middlesex Regiment at 8 p.m. one Company and one Platoon left to garrison posts 2/4 Companies to Billets in ANNEQUIN.	C20
28. — " — ANNEQUIN.	In Billets — Lieut. R.D. Edwards, 3rd Bn reported his arrival from 1st Bn. South Wales Borderers. Three men wounded by shell fire in CUINCHY Post.	C20

Army Form C. 2118.

WAR DIARY
or
INTELLIGENCE SUMMARY.
(Erase heading not required.)

Instructions regarding War Diaries and Intelligence Summaries are contained in F. S. Regs., Part II. and the Staff Manual respectively. Title pages will be prepared in manuscript.

Hour, Date, Place	Summary of Events and Information	Remarks and references to Appendices
29 August 1915 ANNEQUIN	Inskilling - Church parade at 11.0 am. Several officers and orderlies made a reconnaissance of the approaches to the GIVENCHY trenches in the morning.	C/o
30th — GIVENCHY.	Took over GIVENCHY section of trenches from (middlesex) Regiment at 3.p.m. One man wounded.	C/o
31st — " —	Quiet day – at 11:15 p.m. Enemy opened rapid fire, also shelled and bombed the right of our section and the left of the Section on our right. They were eventually silenced by our trench mortars and guns — 3 men wounded.	C/o

BMWilliams
Lieut: Colonel
Comdg. 2nd Bon Roy: Welch Fus:

1st September 1915.

19th Infantry Brigade.
2nd Division.

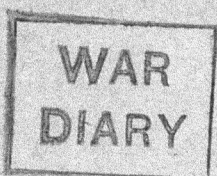

2nd BATTN. THE ROYAL WELSH FUSILIERS.

S E P T E M B E R

1 9 1 5

WAR DIARY
or
INTELLIGENCE SUMMARY.
(Erase heading not required.)

Army Form C. 2118.

Instructions regarding War Diaries and Intelligence Summaries are contained in F.S. Regs., Part II. and the Staff Manual respectively. Title pages will be prepared in manuscript.

Hour, Date, Place		Summary of Events and Information	Remarks and references to Appendices
1st September 1915	CUINCHY.	Working party on Railway Embankment shelled by 50th Battery at 10.30 a.m.	QD
2nd	"	Captain R.H.J. French, 3rd Bn. servant proceeded to join 1st Bn. Royal Welch Fusiliers. - Relieved by Middlesex Regiment at 3p.m. to Billets in ANNEQUIN. - Major General Sir F.Lloyd Colonel of the Regiment came down the trenches and also visited the men when they got in to Billets.	QD
3rd	" ANNEQUIN	In Billets - rainfall day.	QD
4th	" "	Relieved by Royal Berkshire Regiment during afternoon - To Billets in BETHUNE.	QD
5th	" BETHUNE	Battalion on duty up to 12 a.m. Church Parade at 12 noon.	QD
6th	" "	In Billets.	QD
7th	" "	Battalion on duty from 4 p.m. One man killed and one wounded mining.	QD

WAR DIARY
or INTELLIGENCE SUMMARY.
(Erase heading not required.)

Hour, Date, Place	Summary of Events and Information	Remarks and references to Appendices
8. September 1915. BETHUNE.	Lieut. G. McBlain 2nd Bn. Royal Welch Fusiliers and 29 Other ranks joined Battalion (as only joining).	QD
9. "	In billets.	QD
10. "	In billets.	QD
11. "	In billets.	QD
12. "	Four machine gunners arrived from Base. Battalion on duty.	QD
13. "	Relieved the Oxford & Bucks. Buckinghamshire Light Infantry in trenches (B.3.) in front of GIVENCHY.	QD
14. " GIVENCHY.	Germans exploded a mine at 4.45 a.m. Little damage was done – at 8.20 a.m. right company's front line was shelled by trench mortars – at 10.30 a.m. left company shelled by 5.9 Howitzers with high explosive. Casualties – Lieut. D. V. S. Kirkby wounded. Other ranks killed 6 – wounded 15 (5 slightly, 1 at duty).	QD

INTELLIGENCE SUMMARY.

(Erase heading not required.)

Instructions regarding War Diaries and Intelligence Summaries are contained in F.S. Regs., Part II. and the Staff Manual respectively. Title pages will be prepared in manuscript.

Hour, Date, Place	Summary of Events and Information	Remarks and references to Appendices
September 15, 1915. GIVENCHY.	There was an exchange of grenades and trench mortar in front of the night & company during the early morning. Towards midday enemy sent over a few trench mortar shells – Artillery retaliated. One man wounded.	Q.o
16. "	Very quiet night. Front line was trench mortared between 3 p.m. and 3.30 p.m. in retaliation to our shelling. One man killed and one wounded.	Q.o
17. "	Germans exploded a mine at 9.30 a.m. and also at 12.30 p.m. 20 yards of parapet in the towers collapsed otherwise no damage was done – Relieved by 2nd Worcester Regiment at 3.30 p.m. Lo Billets in BETHUNE.	Q.o
18. " BETHUNE.	In Billets.	Q.o
19. "	In Billets.	Q.o
20. "	Relieved Middlesex Regiment in trenches in front of MAISON ROUGE at 4 p.m. Quiet evening.	Q.o

INTELLIGENCE SUMMARY.

(Erase heading not required.)

Instructions regarding War Diaries and Intelligence Summaries are contained in F.S. Regs., Part II. and the Staff Manual respectively. Title pages will be prepared in manuscript.

Hour, Date, Place	Summary of Events and Information	Remarks and references to Appendices
21st September 1915, MAISON ROUGE.	Bombardment of Enemy commenced at 9.30.a.m. and continued during the day and night — Enemy replied with occasional salvos from Field Guns and Howitzers — no hostile rifle or machine gun fire during the night. Our machine guns and look out men kept up fire on enemy's wire and parapets. Major the Hon. E.R. Blagg-Hill D.S.O. wounded — 3 min killed and 3 wounded.	QD
22nd September 1915, MAISON ROUGE.	Bombardment continued — slight reply from enemy. Lieut. H.D.O. Lyle slightly wounded. One killed and 7 wounded.	QD
23rd " "	Bombardment continued — Enemy's retaliation increased slightly. 9th Division and 5th & 6th Brigades made a feint at 4.p.m. we fired rapid for two minutes — enemy made Rifle reply. Coy. Sgt Major Laurie killed, 6 wounded.	QD

INTELLIGENCE SUMMARY.

(Erase heading not required.)

Hour, Date, Place	Summary of Events and Information	Remarks and references to Appendices
14th September 1915 BETHUNE	2nd Bn Welch in BETHUNE - Paraded at 10.45 p.m. and marched into position in assembly trenches front of CAMBRIN.	do
25th CAMBRIN	At 5.50 a.m. moved up in support of 7th Middlesex Regiment. At 6.10 a.m. 7th Middlesex attacked enemy trenches and suffered severely. Two platoons of "B" & "C" Companies advanced to reinforce them and suffered heavy casualties - owing to this the advance was not proceeded with - 2nd Bn Royal Welch Fusiliers took over 1st & 2nd line trenches from 7th Middlesex Regiment. Casualties:— Killed, Capt: A.O. Samson, Capt: J.A. Childe-Freeman & 34 W.O. & O.R. & men. Wounded, Lt.Col. O.de L. Williams D.S.O., Captain E.B. Welton, Lieut: H.bv. Blair, 2nd Lieut: H.C.R. Goldsmith, & 91 N.C.O.s & men. Suffering from Gas Poisoning:- 2nd Lieut: R.H. Drake, Brokman, 3rd Bn East Surrey Regiment (attached) and 4 N.C.O.s & men. Missing 4 men.	do

INTELLIGENCE SUMMARY.

(Erase heading not required.)

Instructions regarding War Diaries and Intelligence Summaries are contained in F. S. Regs, Part II. and the Staff Manual respectively. Title pages will be prepared in manuscript.

Hour, Date, Place	Summary of Events and Information	Remarks and references to Appendices
26th September 1915, CAMBRIN	Continual Bombardment of both sides, troops on our right severely cut up. Casualties:- Killed Captain C.O. Thomas, 1 man, Wounded 7 N.C.O. & men, Suffering from Gas poisoning 1 man.	Q.D
27th " "	Bombardment on both sides - at 5 p.m. attack ordered but as Enemy were holding their trenches in strength we did not proceed with. Casualties:- Wounded 9 N.C.O. & men, Suffering from Gas poisoning 5 N.C.O. & men. 2nd Lieut. J.C. Mann & 35 other Ranks Reinforcements arrived	Q.D
28th " "	Enemys trenches bombarded at intervals during the day. Heavy fighting on our right. - Cleared dead Bodies and removed arms and equipment. Casualties:- 1 man wounded.	Q.D
29th " "	Moderately quiet day - Cleared the dead and removed equipment, &c:- Wet all day. 5th Brigade took over line on our right from 28th Brigade. Casualties: 1 N.C.O. & 1 man wounded. Missing believed killed 1 N.C.O.	Q.D

INTELLIGENCE SUMMARY.

(Erase heading not required.)

Hour, Date, Place	Summary of Events and Information	Remarks and references to Appendices
30th September 1915. CAMBRIN.	Lieut. Colonel O. de L. Williams, D.S.O. rejoined from wounded - quiet day - 5th Scottish Rifles and Middlesex Regiment relieved 5th Brigade. An increase of sniping during the night. 2nd Lieut. W. H. Radford, 2nd R. E. Barnett (9th D. Dewhurst + Lt. W. Smith, 11th Bn. Royal North Lancs. Regiment joined Battalion.	(1)

MMWilliam Lieut. Colonel
Comdg. 2nd Bn. Royal Welch Fusiliers.

In the field
1st October 1915.

19th Infantry Brigade.
2nd Division.

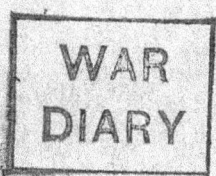

2nd BATTN. THE ROYAL WELCH FUSILIERS.

OCTOBER

1 9 1 5

WAR DIARY or INTELLIGENCE SUMMARY.

(Erase heading not required.)

Army Form C. 2118.

Hour, Date, Place	Summary of Events and Information	Remarks and references to Appendices
1st October 1915, CAMBRIN.	Quiet day – Relieved by 5. Stafford's Regiment and Warwicks at about 5 p.m. To billets in SAILLY LA BOURSE.	M.1.
2nd " SAILLY LA BOURSE.	In Billets – straightening up and re-equipping	M.1.
" " "	Reinforcement of 9 Machine Gunners arrived.	M.1.
3rd " ANNEZIN.	Moved at 1 p.m. to Billets in ANNEZIN.	M.1.
4th " "	In Billets – 11 other Ranks rejoined from 3rd Corps Headquarters	M.1.
5th " "	In Billets – wet all day	M.1.
6th " "	In Billets.	M.1.
7th " "	In Billets. 2nd Lieut W. O. Barry & H. G. Crockett 12th th Bn.	M.1.
" " "	Roy. Welch Fus: reported their arrival, also Boy. gr. br. Sgt. Ward.	M.1.
8th " "	In Billets. 2nd Lieuts R. H. Morris & E. R. J. R. Dolling 12th Bn. Roy. Roy. Welch Fus: reported their arrival – Battalion abroad	M.1.
" " "	to on account of German attack on Hohenzollern.	M.1.
9th " "	In Billets – still standing to.	M.1.
10th " "	In Billets – Church Parade at 10.30 a.m.	M.1.

Forms/C. 2118/11.

Army Form C. 2118.

WAR DIARY
or
INTELLIGENCE SUMMARY.
(Erase heading not required.)

Instructions regarding War Diaries and Intelligence Summaries are contained in F.S. Regs., Part II. and the Staff Manual respectively. Title pages will be prepared in manuscript.

Hour, Date, Place	Summary of Events and Information	Remarks and references to Appendices
11th October 1915. ANNEZIN.	In Billets - Battalion route march of 6 miles	Nil
	Then attacked line of trenches and marched back	Nil
	2 miles to billets.	Nil
12th "	In Billets. Lieut. W.D.G. Tavern, 3rd Bn Roy. Welch	Nil
	Fusrs reported his arrival.	Nil
13th "	In Billets. Wet morning. Stand to ordered	Nil
	from 2 p.m. with orders to be ready to move	Nil
	at 2 hours notice.	Nil
14th "	In Billets.	Nil
15th "	In Billets - 100 other Ranks reinforcements arrived.	Nil
16th " BETHUNE.	Moved from ANNEZIN to BEUVRY. On arrival there	Nil
	found no billets available returned to BETHUNE	
	and billeted near the station.	
	Brigade Headquarters moved up to CAMBRIN, two	
	Battalions in the line in front of MAISON ROUGE.	

Army Form C. 2118.

WAR DIARY
or
INTELLIGENCE SUMMARY.
(Erase heading not required.)

Instructions regarding War Diaries and Intelligence Summaries are contained in F.S. Regs., Part II. and the Staff Manual respectively. Title pages will be prepared in manuscript.

Hour, Date, Place	Summary of Events and Information	Remarks and references to Appendices
17th October 1915. BETHUNE.	In Billets.	Nil.
18. " "	In Billets.	Nil.
19th " "	Moved to Billets in Rue D'Aire.	Nil.
20th " CAMBRIN.	Relieved Middlesex Regiment in trenches in front of Maison Rouge about 3 p.m. Quiet night. 10 Other Ranks rejoined Battalion. 1 man wounded.	Nil.
21st " "	Very quiet day.	Nil.
22nd " "	Quiet day. Machine gunner of the Middlesex (attached) killed. Two minutes combined Field guns, machine gun and rifle fire at 11 p.m. on German wire parties.	Nil.
23rd " "	Captain J. Cuthbert wounded. Captain C. Moody takes over command of "D" Company. At 9 p.m. co-operated with artillery in firing on German working parties for two minutes.	Nil.

WAR DIARY or INTELLIGENCE SUMMARY.

Army Form C. 2118.

(Erase heading not required.)

Hour, Date, Place	Summary of Events and Information	Remarks and references to Appendices
24th October 1915 CAMBRIN.	Quiet day till about 3 p.m. when about 9 heavy shells fell between first and second line trenches on left of line. One man wounded in early morning.	Nil
25th — ANNEQUIN.	Quiet day. Relieved by 1st Batt. Middlesex Regiment at 1 p.m. To Billets in CAMBRIN and ANNEQUIN.	Nil
26th — "	In Billets	Nil
27th — "	In Billets — 200 men on fatigue at CAMBRIN.	Nil
28th — "	In Billets — 200 men on fatigue at CAMBRIN.	Nil
	A little shelling between 4 & 5 p.m. One man wounded. Very wet.	
29th — BUSNETTES.	Moved to billets at BUSNETTES. Arrived 1.15 p.m.	Nil
30th — "	In Billets. 2nd Lieut. H. Mackay joined for duty from West Yorkshire Regiment.	Nil
31 — "	In Billets.	Nil

In the Field,
1st November 1915.

On Divisional ? ? ?
? Comdg. 2nd Bn. Royal Welch Fusiliers

Lieut. Colonel

19th Infantry Brigade.
2nd Division.

(Battn. transferred with
Brigade to 33rd Div.
25.11.15)

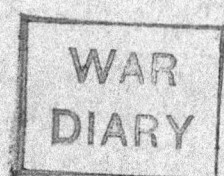

2nd BATTN. THE ROYAL WELCH FUSILIERS.

NOVEMBER

1915

Army Form C. 2118.

WAR DIARY
or
INTELLIGENCE SUMMARY.
(Erase heading not required.)

Instructions regarding War Diaries and Intelligence
Summaries are contained in F.S. Regs., Part II.
and the Staff Manual respectively. Title pages
will be prepared in manuscript.

Hour, Date, Place	Summary of Events and Information	Remarks and references to Appendices
1st November 1915, BUSNETTES	In Billets very wet.	Im R
2nd " "	In Billets. 2nd Lieut. D. Jm. Williams joined for duty.	Im R
3rd " "	In Billets.	Im R
4th " "	In Billets. Commanding Officer's Parade - Route march.	Im R
5th " BETHUNE.	Moved at 2 p.m. to Billets in RUE D'AIRE, BETHUNE.	Im R
6th " CAMBRIN.	Moved to support line in Harley St. Cambrin Support Point, Braddell Point Cambrin Group Port Fives arriving 1.30 pm. 2nd day Relieved Royal Berks.	Im R
7th " "	Remained in support line. Working parties bricking and improving communication trenches. Captain Harrison Medical Officer left for 19th Field Ambulance. Lieut. Dunn relieved him.	Im R
8th " "	Support Line - same work continued.	Im R
9th " "	Support Line - same work continued.	Im R
10th " "	Support Line - same work continued.	Im R

WAR DIARY
or
INTELLIGENCE SUMMARY.

(Erase heading not required.)

Army Form C. 2118.

Instructions regarding War Diaries and Intelligence Summaries are contained in F.S. Regs., Part II. and the Staff Manual respectively. Title pages will be prepared in manuscript.

Hour, Date, Place		Summary of Events and Information	Remarks and references to Appendices
10th November 1915	CAMBRIN	Six heavy shells on PONT FIXÉ about 1 yard - Bright in officers' mess. One servant slightly wounded.	Im 1
11th	"	Suffert Line. Few heavy shells all the afternoon	Im 1
12th	"	About 500 heavy shells fell round PONT FIXÉ. No casualties.	Im 1
	"	Support Line.	
13th	CAMBRIN	Relieved at 10.30 a.m. by 2nd Queens. Ok 4.15 re-lieved 7th Queens in Z.1. Sect.	Im 1
14th	"	Cleaning up trenches. Weather better. About small shells dropped in rear of support line. Frost at night.	Im 1
15th	"	Quiet day except for intermittent shelling 2 men wounded and one man killed.	Im 1
16th	"	Intermittent shelling during the day. Somewhat shelling during the evening.	Im 1
17th	"	Quiet day. One man wounded in the evening - Wet night.	Im 1

WAR DIARY
or
INTELLIGENCE SUMMARY.

(Erase heading not required.)

Army Form C. 2118.

Hour, Date, Place	Summary of Events and Information	Remarks and references to Appendices
November 18/15 CAMBRIN.	Quiet day.	Nil
19th " BEVRY.	9.a.m. "D" Company relieved by 2nd Argyll and Sutherland Highlanders. 10.a.m. Battalion relieved by 5th Scottish Rifles. "A", "C", "D" Companies to Billets in BEVRY. "B" Company remaining in dug-outs at MAISON ROUGE.	
20th " "	In Billets.	Nil
21st " "	Relieved by S.G.D. and moved to fresh Billets at GONNEHEM arriving 2.30 p.m. Time Out cold.	Nil
22nd " "	In Billets. Drums beat 3.45 p.m.	Nil
23rd " "	In Billets.	Nil
24th " "	In Billets. 2nd Lieuts Craig & Higginson rejoined.	Nil
25th " "	In Billets. Armoons 9. Brigade transferred from 2nd to 3.3rd Divisions.	Nil
26th " "	Captains Edwards and Graves rejoined from St Pol.	Nil
27th " "	In Billets.	Nil

WAR DIARY
INTELLIGENCE SUMMARY.
(Erase heading not required.)

Army Form C. 2118.

Hour, Date, Place	Summary of Events and Information	Remarks and references to Appendices
26th November 1915. GONNEHEM.	In billets.	Nil
29th " OBLINGHEM.	Moved to fresh billets at OBLINGHEM. Arrived 2nd Lieuts. Townsend, Barrett, Corning and Morgan.	Nil Nil
30th "	In billets.	

For Lt. Col. ——
Lieut. Colonel
Comdg. 2nd Bn. Senr. Royal Welch Fusiliers.

In the Field,
1st December 1915.

19 INFANTRY BRIGADE.
2 BN ARGYLE & SOUTHERL
HIGHLANDERS.
1 BN MIDDLESEX REGIMEN
2 BN ROYAL WELSH FUS
1914 AUG TO 1915 NOV.

1365

www.ingramcontent.com/pod-product-compliance
Lightning Source LLC
Chambersburg PA
CBHW081433160426
43193CB00013B/2267